The Art of Empowering Children

A Karate Master's Secrets

by

John C. Graybeal

First printing 1998.
Second printing 1999.

ISBN 1-889309-00-1
CIP 98-070004

www.empwr.com

Cover Design by: Dana Reischauer
Cover Photography by: Eliseo Valdes
Edited by: Rebecca Ewert Schaefer

Attention Organizations and Schools:

Quantity discounts are available for bulk purchases of this book for educational purposes or fund raising. Special books or book excerpts can also be created to fit specific needs.

For information, please contact Empower Press toll free 888-663-9565 or visit our web page at www.empwr.com.

TABLE OF CONTENTS

Graybeal

Acknowledgments

I look upon everything I do with great excitement and passion, and this book is no exception. It came together with the help of many wonderful people. Indeed, many more thanks are appropriate than can be conveyed on the printed page.

Thanks to my parents, Irene and Richard, who gave me a life that most only dream of. Thanks to my father for his quest for perfection and his constant drive to make me better—I will never forget, your wisdom. Thanks to my mother who showed me that the little things do count.

To my staff at Martial Arts America, thanks for taking care of the details as my mind raced forward searching for more answers and finding more questions. Your support offered me the chance to pursue my greatest dreams.

To my martial arts teacher, John F. Penn: The gift you gave me built the foundation for this book and many more. You instilled in me the determination to get up no matter how many times I was knocked down.

There are many mentors in my life, and I thank you all, especially Larry Alvey, Dr. Larry Miller, and Master Hank Giles. Your guidance continues to lead me toward a powerful future.

To my coaches, Dr. Jan Elfline and Sheren Spence Frame: your direction through the process of learning illuminated me; your words gave me energy and kept me on track.

To my constant pal, Wind River's Boot Lace CDX

Graybeal

JH KGC—AKA "Lacey the Wonder Dog:" Your understanding and intelligence give me comfort every minute of the day. Allowing me to escape in your companionship is irreplaceable.

To my friends, Fred Mertens, Rick Bell, Andrew Wood, and Larry Doke: Thank you. Your insistence that I sit at the computer spurred me forward toward the vision. You helped me and can do the same for others.

To the many martial arts instructors with whom I have been fortunate to train over the past years: Our mutual efforts to push each other to higher levels will forever be etched in my mind.

To the many students I have been fortunate to teach: Without you there would be no school or martial arts in my life. You have touched my heart. Always remember, I will be there for you.

And finally thanks to the many parents, friends, and others behind the scenes who provided me the opportunity to work with children.

I can't thank everyone enough for your patience and time. You are all "Super Black Belts."

Dedication

To everyone who teaches children:

You are the ones who shape our future.

Preface

On a cold January morning I sat at a stop light, my truck engine idling, watching the snow piling up outside. The pure white flakes stuck to everything and enhanced each curve and line they touched. They scattered across the window, followed by the windshield wipers clearing a path. When the light turned green, my foot moved off the brake and I felt my tires slip, much like my own life slipping from one thing to the next. I shifted into four wheel drive. The gears caught, and I felt the wheels correct.

In recent days I had been asking myself many questions. What would I be doing next week, next year? What would cause me to go this way or that? Instead of waiting to see what would happen, why couldn't I make things happen the way I wanted? How could I insure that I was playing to win, rather than simply playing not to lose? I was doing what I loved, but not to the extent I wanted. I was letting other forces push me, causing my life to slip just like the tires. I knew I had the pieces to the puzzle of life—teaching, working with children, and writing—they just weren't assembled correctly.

The windshield wipers again cleared their path, and I thought of all the irrelevant events I had allowed to pile up, blocking my goals like the snow in front of my truck. "*A fighter jet doesn't need windshield wipers,*" I thought, going back to my years as a pilot. Nothing sticks to it as it speeds toward its destination. I wanted to be like that fighter jet. I wanted to pierce through the unimportant things toward my own destiny—a task requiring perception, planning, and focus.

In grade school I remember my parents and teachers were concerned about my inability to focus. I recall a "special teacher" pulling me out of class and taking me for hearing and vision tests. She showed up once a week and took students to the "round room." The round room was about twelve feet in diameter and painted cream to match the asbestos on the ceiling. It was just around the corner from the principal's office, a place no student wanted to go. I sat there and listened to beep after beep, then read letter after letter. One by one I aced each test, leaving everyone confused. If it wasn't my hearing or vision, what was it? Why was I having so much trouble? Did I have what we now call Attention Deficit Disorder? Back in the early 70's they called it "all boy," "hyperactive," or "active imagination."

Some never returned from the round room, as they were shuffled off to other classrooms or special schools. But I returned, and my troubles continued. One afternoon I eavesdropped as my teacher complained to my mother: "Why is he not listening to me? He has the ability; he just isn't using it." I went through most of my childhood hearing the same thing over and over. "He has the ability...if he would only try."

It wasn't until I took martial arts lessons in the fall of my sophomore year that I first began to understand my own potential. I began a new understanding of life—or what could be understood about life at the ripe old age of fifteen. Suddenly I had physical confidence and the ability to change the way I communicated within my own mind. It's quite a motivator to stay focused when someone is kicking and punching at your head. I learned to focus through martial arts and one by one my "troubles" began to disappear. My grades began to climb and so did my ambitions. I began to dream, not only about tomorrow, but about the next month and the next year. I had become empowered.

On that snowy January day, years later, I parked my truck and walked across the lot toward my martial arts school. The children were just arriving and it hit me: My next step, this book.

I've collected many stories since I began teaching martial arts, and this book recalls a few. During college I began teaching a children's class at the local YMCA on Friday evenings. As the classes grew, so did I, not only in the way I taught, but in the way I learned. When I opened my own martial arts school in 1993, it was a selfish act in which I thought only of the joy I would receive from teaching. Now I work with more than two hundred children each week. It is rewarding and challenging—and something I'm compelled to share.

A mentor recently asked me what I wanted to leave the world.

Without hesitating, I answered, "I'd like to impact a million children...just as my teachers have impacted me."

"It is the supreme art of the teacher to awaken joy in creative expression and knowledge."
—Albert Einstein

Introduction
Who, What, When, and Why

"There is nothing either good or bad, but thinking makes it so."
—William Shakespeare

WHO IS THIS BOOK FOR?

Our future is our children, and we all have the opportunity to empower them. Without question, parents play a major role in the lives of children, but they aren't the only ones. Schoolteachers impact children daily, but they are not the only ones who teach. Coaches guide children, but they are not the only ones who coach. We all must assume responsibility for shaping our future by shaping our children. This book offers techniques I've used which relate to any environment where adults interact with children, and the desired outcome is a child enlightened with knowledge, skills, and experiences.

Webster's dictionary defines *teach* as:
To show or help a person to learn to do
And defines *empower* as:
To give power or authority to; or enable or permit

This book is for all of us. If you have ever shown someone something, you are a teacher. If you have ever given a lesson, you are a teacher. If you have ever provided insight, you are a teacher. If someone has ever followed your example, you are a teacher. Each of us, every day, is a teacher. Accept the role as a teacher and you can change the world.

"You can have everything in life you want, if you will just help enough other people get what they want."
—Zig Ziglar

WHAT IS IT ABOUT?

Over the years, I have witnessed mistakes made by coaches, parents, and teachers. And I must admit, I have made plenty of my own. Most are simple errors that are easy to fix, but a few instill undesirable characteristics and undesirable traits. As I share my thoughts, remember the most important techniques are those that come from within yourself, those with which you are confident, those you understand. Teaching is not a science; it's an art.

One of my closest friends often reminds me, "You know what you know; you know what you don't know. But it's what you *don't know* you don't know that holds you back." As you read this book, you might find out something you didn't know you didn't know. I learn something new every day, and I love it when I get to share new information with people. I hope each day I am able to teach a child something new that she will remember for the rest of her life.

WHEN?

Every teacher wants to be better, but some find it difficult to take the first step. Busy schedules and little time can sabotage the best intentions. Resolve right now to be different—because you are different. Start with one skill, and when you master that, move on to another.

Now is the best time to start learning how to empower children, and don't stop until you have. At our school we have five concepts that represent martial arts excellence: **Courtesy, Integrity, Perseverance, Self-Control, Indomitable Spirit**.

My lessons often focus on perseverance, and now I ask you to focus on perseverance also.

WHY IS EMPOWERING IMPORTANT?

Before our martial arts students are promoted from one belt color to the next, we send a letter asking parents and teachers if the student is continuing the spirit of martial arts outside the studio. In other words, is he or she exhibiting focus, self-control, effort, and courtesy? A few years ago, I received a negative report. The teacher stated that five year old Joey was not conducting himself well, "...his behavior forces me to not recommend promotion." The mother echoed similar concerns, "It's his behavior..."

The next afternoon I asked Joey into the conference room. He climbed up on a chair and faced me across the table.

"Do you know why you are not going to be promoted?" I asked as he stared back with his large brown eyes.

"Because I'm bad."

"Well, it's not that you are bad; it's that sometimes you don't choose the best actions. Do you know what you're going to have to do to be promoted to your next belt?"

"Be good."

"You are a good boy, very good. Can you think of any specific things that happened this week that are keeping your teacher from recommending you for promotion?"

"I was bad."

I changed my words, "Can you tell me something you do that is good behavior?"

"I just have to be good."

"Can you tell me something you did that is not so good? Something you did that wasn't okay?"

Joey sat there for a few seconds and then repeated, "I've got to be good, not bad."

This five-year-old had no idea what constituted "good" or "bad" behavior. He'd been told he was bad so often that he'd come to believe it. I spent the next half hour explaining and convincing him he was good, though sometimes his behavior left a bit to be desired. I made an impassioned speech about how very special he was to me and to the other instructors. Later, I phoned the teacher and told her what he'd said.

To this she replied, "Maybe that's why he says he wants to kill himself."

My chin hit the floor. This child was convinced he was bad, so bad he wanted to kill himself!

Joey's teacher was contributing to programming his mind with messages about his behavior, but not providing him with any skills to change. She was not moving him forward. Regardless of anything else she may have done in the classroom, she was definitely employing non-empowering techniques in this situation. I often think of Joey and wonder what will happen to him as he grows up? Will he become empowered and successful? Or is he destined to fall short of his full potential?

I can't help but compare him to Andrew, a bright young sixteen year old who carried himself as if he were several years older. He held a part-time job at my martial arts school as an assistant instructor. One Tuesday evening as he headed to work, he came to a halt behind several cars stopped at a green light.

"What's taking these guys so long?" he asked himself. Then he saw the hold up—a car crash. He turned off the engine and raced toward the scene. A blue mini-van had hit a Cutlass broadside. The driver of the mini-van stood motionless, inspecting the damage to his car as three bystanders struggled to open the other driver's door.

One of those who ran to help, a middle-aged woman, yelled from inside the car: "He's not breathing!"

"Somebody call 911!" an older man shouted.

Andrew took action. He reached inside the Cutlass, pulled the driver out, and laid him on the ground. When he found no pulse, he began CPR. He was able to feel a faint heartbeat as the rescue squad arrived.

Andrew was empowered. He was secure and confident in himself and his abilities. No one can say with certainty when he began to feel this way, but the teachers in his life—including his parents, relatives, coaches, and friends—empowered him to save a man's life and go on to the success he's achieved today.

This book is about empowering children as Andrew was empowered. Some children, like Andrew, are directed toward success while others, like Joey, are directed elsewhere. I want every child to grow up able to make empowered decisions like Andrew did. As adults, we can empower children to respond in healthy and positive ways to the events that occur around them. We can empower them on a level that insures successful accomplishment of their greatest—and smallest—desires and goals. It all starts with the little bits of information we give them every time we make contact. Often adults decide (either consciously or not) that a child won't amount to much, and they treat them based on that thought. I believe children will rise to the expectations we have for them.

Throughout this book, I use examples from my martial arts school. It is what I have the most experience with. I have also used these same techniques in the park or gym. They are not martial arts techniques— they are empowering techniques that work anywhere.

Chapter One

Class Line-Up

"Sure I am of this, that you have only to endure to conquer. You have only to persevere to save yourselves."
—Sir Winston Churchill

I arrived at the martial arts school early one morning and noticed a small envelope on my desk. One of my students, who was also one of my martial arts instructors, had recently graduated from high school. I recognized his handwriting and expected a thank you note for the small gift I'd sent. When I opened it I found much more!

Dear Mr. Graybeal,

Your card was very inspirational, just as you have been to me for many years. I have grown up admiring you as a role model. I have learned a great deal from you, and you have given me so much. You have been a hero to me, giving me the skills and shaping my character into what it is today. You have given me the opportunities to have succeeded as I have done and to go on to even better things. I will try to live up to your teachings and expectations of me.

Perhaps the greatest thing you have given me is the ability and opportunity to give back to other children some of what you have given me. I've been able to work with hundreds of children whom I love and adore, and I hope that I've been able to make a difference in their lives as well. I've come to learn that every single student I work with is very special and deserves the best. I hope that part of what I give them helps to make them the best that they can possibly be. Thank you for making me the young man that I am, and I wish you luck in shaping the lives of others as I try to pass on what you have given me.

Jeff

I stood frozen, not knowing whether to cry or smile. Out of thousands of students, Jeff had been with me the longest, from the time he was five. He had seen me change as much as I had seen him change. And he reflected the very personal empowerment I wanted to accomplish with my life and my teaching. This letter confirmed in my mind that what I was doing worked, and brought with it an overwhelming feeling I carry with me every day.

Note in hand, I caught myself staring out the window, remembering a similar letter I'd written to my own martial arts instructor when I graduated from high school. I wanted nothing more than to live up to what he believed I could be. What was passed on to me I now had passed on to another. He, in turn, will pass it on as well.

Isn't life grand?

A WORD TO TEACHERS

Before we begin our journey, we must start with ourselves. As adults, we not only need to mold the lives of our students, but we must continually mold our own.

WRITTEN GOALS

I have read statistics that only five percent of the population have defined goals, and of those, only one percent actually write those goals on paper. A famous story about the 1953 graduating class at Yale University illustrates this point well. At graduation, a researcher gathered the class together and asked how many people had goals and how many had those goals written down so they could refer to them. Twenty years later, the researcher interviewed them again and found that the three percent with written goals had more personal wealth and personal success than the rest of the class combined.

My goal in September of 1993 was to have two hundred students at the martial arts school. On a piece of paper I wrote "200 students," and taped it to my bathroom mirror. Every day I would wake and see "200 students." Eighteen months later I had two hundred students, and I removed the piece of paper from my mirror. Nine months later I still had two hundred students. I realized there might be something to writing down goals. I took another piece of paper and wrote "400 students." It went on my bathroom mirror. Six months into the new goal, I had 280 students.

When you make a commitment to change, to take

action, write your goals on a piece of paper. Put it where you can see it every day. Decide now what you want from yourself and what you want from your future.

Oh, Yes You Can!

I sat across the table from a father whose son, Aaron, wanted to quit taking martial arts lessons. The "full of energy" ten year old had been taking lessons for two years, and out of the blue his father ended up in my conference room explaining a difficult situation. Mr. Thomas repeated over and over how he loved the program and thought it was beneficial to Aaron.

"Can you see how this (martial arts) will improve his life?" I asked.

"Oh, yes, I have seen great improvements." He leaned back in the chair, then forward, resting his elbows on the table.

"Then, why are you letting him quit?"

"He doesn't want to do it anymore. I can't force him." He shifted again and folded his arms.

"Sure you can, you're the father," I said, doing my best to use a voice that was non-confrontational.

"I suppose I could, but I'm not going to."

"What would happen if you did?"

"I'm not going to, so it doesn't matter." He cleared his throat and looked down at the table.

"I know you're not going to, but what if you did? You said the program was beneficial and you thought he was getting a great deal out of it. What would happen if you forced him to continue?"

Mr. Thomas had difficulty imagining himself forcing his child to come to class. In his mind, I assume "forcing" involved an image of dragging a kicking and screaming ten year old into the martial arts school. In my mind, it meant encouragement and motivation.

When parents don't see the true benefit of a program or activity, they often say they can't force their child. When they do see the benefit, they often ask for help in providing motivation.

I often speak with people who are quick to accept failure, or others who are quick to accept average instead of striving for excellence. They'll say, "You can't be perfect." And I always answer, "Why not? What if you consistently aimed for perfection? What would be different in your life?"

I constantly ask myself these questions. What if I wrote a book that would help people work with children? What if I asked people questions that provoked them into thinking about possibilities and not self-imposed limiting beliefs? What if I changed the way I thought and became an outstanding teacher?

**"The countenances of children, like those of animals, a re masks, not faces, for they have not yet developed a significant profile of their own."
—W. H. Auden**

FIVE STEPS TO SUCCESS

One afternoon I sat in my office watching an instructor lead class. I knew he was having difficulties in other areas of his life. Being one to always offer encouragement toward goals, I turned my chair around, fired up the computer, and typed "Martial Arts America's Five Steps to Success" across the top of the page. This list still hangs in my office:

Action
Change
Communication
Responsibility
Knowledge

Action

Before you finish any task, you must first begin. You begin by taking action. You could write a few notes, read a book, or go to the library—anything that will move you forward.

Our goal is to increase our level of communication with children, and as usual, the most difficult step is the first. I once had an adult student who faced a dilemma about her future, in particular where she wanted to live. She could not decide whether to stay in Illinois or move to Las Vegas where her parents lived. One night she walked into the school with a long face and arms hanging limp at her side. I asked her into the office, and we talked for some time about taking action. We even wrote down a few goals. The next morning I received a phone call. She was packing as we spoke, heading for the desert.

Nike's famous slogan, "Just do it," is an extremely powerful message. Just do it—do *something*. Often *anything* is better than just sitting on the couch. As the old saying goes, be the kind of person who makes things happen, or at the very least, the kind of person who is there when it happens. What you don't want to be is the kind of person who sits and wonders what happened.

I lead a very busy and often hectic life, one in which

I have little spare time. I prepare myself each day to take action and move forward toward my goals.

Change

If the action you take doesn't work, then change. It sounds simple, and it is. If that new action doesn't work? Change again. The ability to look upon a situation and change the perspective gives you power. Start by changing your daily routine. Small changes will lead to powerful ones.

"Life is measured by the rapidity of change, the succession of influences that modify the being."
—George Eliot

Paul, a friend of mine, spent a few years traveling the country consulting with martial arts school owners. He had one goal in mind—increasing their business. He set up a meeting with the owner of a martial arts school in New York City. Upon his arrival, he spent a few minutes getting acquainted and then went into the office to discuss business. The school owner began to talk about how bad business was.

"People just aren't coming in," the owner complained.

"How many calls did you make last night to prospective students?"

"Ten."

"Could you make fifteen tonight?"

"Yeah, I suppose."

"Could you make twenty?" Paul asked, lowering his voice.

"Maybe."

"Could you make thirty?"

"No. That would take too long. I like to be home by 9:00."

With that Paul reached across the desk and extended his fingers to represent a gun. "If I held a gun to your head do you think you could make those thirty calls?"

"Yes," the owner said nervously.

Paul leaned back in his chair. "Well, I can't hold a gun to your head, but you can!"

Sometimes we just need motivation.

Most people who work with children are entrenched in the techniques they grew up with. Some work and some don't. The best teachers I know move rapidly from one technique to the next in order to reach each student. To empower children, you must be willing to change techniques.

Communication

There are two types of communication: internal and external. Your internal communication is the voice inside your head, and your external communication is how you sound, stand, and move. Powerful internal communication leads to powerful external communication. If you give yourself an empowering message before you work with a child, chances are you'll give that same message to him.

Responsibility

Working with many great leaders in the civilian and military world, I have learned that great leaders are quick to stand up and take responsibility. For many people it seems natural to shift the blame to others. Don't fall into that trap. Take responsibility for your words and actions, and teach your students to do the same. When you instill in a child the need to take responsibility for everything in his life, you give him the key to his own success.

Knowledge

There is no such thing as useless information. Every bit of knowledge you bring into your mind will move you forward. As the information age we live in grows and expands, we find knowledge in many types of media: computers, the Internet, television, videos, audio tapes, and perhaps the most important vehicle for information, the printed word. Enjoy books and gain information, all types of information, and you will enhance your communication with your students.

"When you're tough on yourself, life is going to be infinitely easier on you."
—Zig Ziglar

TEACHING IMPACT

In college my *Literature of the Bible* professor, Dr. Herbert, left a lasting impression that impacts my interpretation of every book I read. I remember seeing him run down the hallway into our small yellow room and throw himself into his chair exactly as the second hand swept past twelve. This large man would wipe small beads of perspiration from his forehead, flip open the Old Testament, and without taking a breath, read a verse from Genesis in perfect Old English. The way he commanded our attention was riveting. He spoke of history and tradition as it related to the Bible. He challenged every one of us in that room to search for our own interpretation of exactly what each verse meant.

Likewise, it was apparent to me, then and now, that my third grade teacher, Mrs. Ropp, cared deeply about her students. The way she talked to us and touched our lives still brings a smile to my face. Every time I visit one of my karate students at her school I say hi and tell her what a wonderful job she did teaching me. But it isn't just schoolteachers I remember. I also recall my martial arts teacher, my first flying instructor, and others who made an impact on my life. All these people gave me something that empowered my life. Just as these individuals shaped my life, you're shaping the future of others with whom you make contact.

Throughout this book, I refer to success as the quality actions that produce more for children as they grow up and more for the lives of others once they reach adulthood in terms of happiness, satisfaction, and reward. There are many ways to interpret what success is, and no two may be alike. This book is not written to apply my standards for success to everyone; it is written to allow everyone to learn to apply their own.

A friend of mine who owns a martial arts school in Chicago sent me an advertisement he was working on. There was a picture of a martial arts instructor handing a student a belt. The headline read:

Integrity: Because it Doesn't Happen by Accident

He's right. Values and the traits that support values don't happen by accident. They are instilled through constant effort. People often talk about values as if they are something you pick up at the store. They are not commodities, but are the intrinsic qualities that make our world better. And you can make an impact on your students, empowering them with intrinsic qualities that will shape your future and theirs.

Chapter Two

Climb Aboard

"Teaching is not a lost art, but the regard for it is a lost tradition."
—Jacques Barzun

FOR A CHILD TO LEARN

There are several keys to creating a productive learning atmosphere. **Structure, focus, discipline**, and **respect** are four elements teachers must control in order to empower their students. The physical location is not as important as what teachers do with their surroundings. Whether you teach in a small quiet room, on a sailboat, or on the side of a mountain, these four elements can afford you the opportunity to reach your students.

Structure

Structure is the way in which the learning environment is arranged and of what the atmosphere consists. Have you ever watched a little league field in complete chaos or entered a classroom and found the students totally out of control? My martial arts school operates at a fast pace. At 3:20 p.m. the doors fly open and children ages three to fifteen rush in. At first you might think you're in danger of being trampled, but on second look, you would see the students immediately settle and begin learning. We are able to conduct productive classes in part because we demand a highly structured atmosphere.

In the Air Force, combat is chaotic. Without structure the teamwork necessary to complete each task would be nonexistent. Without structure there would be no excitement in watching a football game. In our school children must understand what we expect. Beginning with their first class, our instructors explain everything in detail: The way to wear the uniform, the way to talk to the instructors, the way to stand, and the way to move. The instructors watch students every minute to insure they follow the guidelines. If the students forget, the instructors remind them. This approach allows us to create an environment devoted to learning because we tell them what we expect.

Remember the chaos on the baseball field? It happens when players don't know what the coaches expect. No one has taught them what to do while they're out on the field. One of the best ways to establish structure is to tell the students what you expect and then nurture them to a point where they are able to understand and apply that knowledge.

Focus

Perhaps you've watched a television that uses tinfoil for an antenna. At times the picture becomes so fuzzy and out of focus that concentration is impossible. The same thing happens when a teacher fails to focus on the needs of the students. The students can't concentrate. The teacher may be coming in so fuzzy and out of focus that the students' minds wander.

Strong leadership skills are critical in a learning environment. Assert yourself as the one in control by using a commanding voice and a presence that non-verbally communicates that you are the leader. These simple things help bring the minds of the students in line for learning. And remember, the more slack you allow your students, the more slack they will take. Sooner or later every student will test his teacher to see what is permissible and what is not. Be relentless in your pursuit of the ideal learning environment.

Each and every student needs a different environment. Some of my students focus better with the stereo on. Others focus better when I move at a fast pace. As teachers we must remove distractions from some students' immediate surroundings and place stimulants in others'. A physiologist told me a wonderful story about a young man who listened attentively to the teacher when he was shredding paper at his desk, but was less attentive when he did not have paper to shred. He was kinesthetic and needed paper to shred to take up some of his energy so he could focus on the teacher's words! Your students will let you know what they need. We only need to listen and then take action.

Discipline

The word "discipline" often conjures up unpleasant thoughts. Sometimes when I've mentioned to parents that "I'm going to increase the discipline" with their son or daughter, I've had to explain that I don't mean punishment. When successful martial arts students walk through the doors of the school, they come to attention and bow respectfully to the first instructor they see. This discipline sets the pace for the entire session. By conducting our classes in a regimented and disciplined manner, the instructors are able to become more efficient in their teaching. The students know where to go and what to do. The teachers are able to cover more information, knowing that when their backs are turned the students continue to perform as expected.

When our students step onto the training floor, they sit with their feet crossed, hands on their knees, and their backs straight as arrows. When instructed to stand up they answer, "yes, sir" or "yes, ma'am" and spring to stand at attention. The instructor invites them to line up, and the students run to their positions and await further commands.

The reason for this is simple. If we run an undisciplined school, students can fill their heads with different options. They can sit with feet out, sit with hands in front or behind, lie on their stomachs, or lie on their backs. We want the students to learn to make the correct decisions when they have the chance. This type of guidance requiring adherence to strict rules helps them develop decision-making skills. Our students focus on the tasks at hand and do not venture off searching for choices, distracting them from the teacher and the lesson.

I hear from parents all the time that their child has a problem "staying on task." This is code for an undisciplined teacher. The learning rule "Primacy" is that people are more likely to remember what they learn first. If the first thing a student learns is to "stay on task," then staying on task will be ingrained in him. The mother of a ten year old recently gave me this personal journal entry. Her son has been involved in martial arts classes about four months:

"I go to karate after school. Karate has fun skills you can learn. You learn forms and other self-defense. If you bring in a friend you can get a flag patch.

Here we are at Bloomington, at Martial Arts America. First you go in and dress. Then you come out and bow to the flag before you get on the mat. Then you sit down with your back straight, legs crossed, and hands on your knees. When it's time for class your instructor says to stand up, and then you give him your attendance card. And now when he says your belt, you line up on the black mark. After class you bow to the instructor and clap your hands and then when he says, "You're dismissed," you run and before you get off the mat you bow to the flag and wait for your dad or mom. Then you go back home.

We did kicks, punches, and blocks in class. Sometimes we do the Chicken Drill, which is when you hold one leg and put one hand in your belt and hop around and try to knock people down with your arm still in your belt. And we also do the Tiger Drill, which is when you stand on some kind of line and put both hands in your belt and try to knock people off the line without knocking yourself off. And we also do Arrow Storm where the instructor shoots an arrow at you. And that is my journal for today.

Mission accomplished, for this young student has a clear understanding of what is expected of him. The guidelines we offer in class have been explained and understood. This student is successful at martial arts because we have been able to give him focus. Take out a piece of paper, outline the procedures for your students, explain to them what is expected, and watch them learn.

Can you have too much discipline? No. In all the years I have been teaching martial arts, no one has ever come to me and said they were quitting because there was too much discipline.

I once asked several parents a question, "Can you think of any other activities that provide children with the type of discipline we have at our school?"

They all answered, "no." But this type of discipline can be in any activity.

Discipline is a wonderful thing when it is administered in a warm and caring environment.

Respect

A mother came to me and asked me to speak with her son, Brandon, who was having difficulty in school. She sat down at the conference table and used the following as an example. "When a teacher tells him the sky is blue, he answers, 'No, it's green.' If the teacher tells him two plus two equals four, he walks away upset. He struggles with everything the teacher says. What do you think is going on?"

We talked for a while, and in the course of the conversation I learned that he went to a school in which the students called the teachers by their first names (Mary instead of Mrs. Doe). The school's philosophy was that students and teachers were on the same level. I asked the mother the next logical question. "If the students and the teachers are on the same level, who is teaching whom? And how can you expect a child to learn if he doesn't hold the teacher in high regard?" I then asked why her son calls her "Mom" instead of "Karen?" This line of questioning produced an intriguing discussion, one we continued off and on for several days as we determined exactly what respect really was. Is it a title like simply referring to a teacher as Mr. or Mrs.? Or is it something more? There must be a hierarchical relationship between a teacher and a student in order to establish the protocols for the interaction between the two. One of the easiest ways to do this is to use titles.

I am first to admit that sometimes I am uncomfortable referring to myself as Mr. Graybeal or Master Graybeal. During a staff meeting I assigned a project to one of my instructors to see if he could correlate student retention to the way students referred to the instructors. The next meeting he returned with a list of current students and students who quit. We spent several hours logging how each student addressed us. We found that of the students who quit, either they or their parents had addressed the instructors by their first names. Nearly all of the current students and parents refer to the instructors as "Mr." or "Mrs."

By referring to someone formally, a professional relationship is developed, and respect is increased.

A father came to me the other day and complimented me on how I demand respect from the students. At first I was taken aback. I sure didn't feel I "demanded" respect. In fact, I'd always heard that one who demands respect is likely to be treated with animosity. I thought about that for several days. That father was correct. I do demand respect, and after further consideration I determined that it is perfectly acceptable to do so. Done properly in a caring, nurturing manner, students will respond in a way that is a reflection of who the teacher is and how he or she behaves.

While student and teacher have distinct roles,

mutual respect is a must to strengthen the foundation for learning. The teacher must place the student at a specific level, whether that student is his son or daughter or someone he has never met.

"A schoolmaster should have an atmosphere of awe, and walk wonderingly, as if he was amazed at being himself."
—Walter Bagehot

THE SUPPORT TRIANGLE

A child's life has many components, and it's up to the adults to help that child understand how those components fit together. Who takes any given role in the student's life and how that role relates to other role models correlates directly to the empowerment of a student. A schoolteacher can be more effective if the parents are supportive of her efforts. If a schoolteacher is supportive of what takes place in our martial arts class, the student receives the maximum benefit both places.

The Support Triangle is a simplified visual representation of how I like to arrange three main teaching forces.

Each side of the triangle represents a vital role in the development of a child. Communication between all three sides should be constant in order to gain the maximum teaching benefits.

Each element must enhance and challenge the student on an individual basis and should support the other two elements. The below example contains the parents, the schoolteacher, and the martial arts teacher.

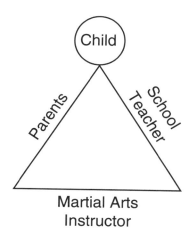

The third element should incorporate a year-long activity into the Support Triangle. I prefer to see physically empowering activities like martial arts since physical ability is often overlooked. This doesn't mean that all children need to become Olympic-caliber athletes, but they need to feel comfortable about how they use their bodies. Giving a child a physical skill helps increase self-confidence and creates a more successful future.

By identifying the relationship between the people who work together in creating a successful and empowered child, we can enhance not only our own position but the position of others.

TEACHING PRINCIPLES

Several years ago Mr. Fred Mertens, an experienced martial arts instructor, identified five elements needed to transform his students into successful adults.

Those five elements became known as The Teaching Principles:

Caring, Belief, Challenge, Reward, Praise.

Caring

Children have the wonderful ability to wear their hearts on their sleeves, something we seem to lose as we age. Your students will sense if you care about what you are doing and if you care about them. If you don't care about your students, you shouldn't expect quality learning.

"People seldom see the halting and painful steps by which the most insignificant success is achieved."
—Anne Sullivan

I have been able to work with every child that has entered my school, no matter how "difficult" he or she was perceived to be. Why? I care. Some are more reluctant than others, and some I'm only able to engage in conversation, but they know I care. Parents are the same way. When a parent comes into my school, they're more concerned that I will care about their son or daughter than the fact that I was a United States martial arts champion, an F-16 fighter pilot, or an author.

When I meet a new student, I drop everything. I want him to know from the moment we meet that I care about him. I learn his name—and remember it. I start asking questions: his age, the name of his family's pet, his brothers or sisters...I establish an open line of communication that conveys my true sense of caring.

Belief

Belief in your students can make the difference between empowerment and shattered confidence. When young students join my program I ask the parent(s) about the child's overall physical condition. I ask about any potentially dangerous limitations, but I avoid learning other limiting beliefs adults may have thrust upon the child.

A parent once told me that her son, Ryan, couldn't sit still in a class for over thirty minutes. "At thirty-one minutes he loses all focus and concentration. It's okay to tell him to leave when he loses it."

How would you react knowing this?

It's not the first time Ryan loses focus that concerns most teachers. They will work with great enthusiasm to focus his attention. But after the fifth or sixth time it almost seems right to accept what the mother said, though in doing so it's possible we only encourage the negative behavior.

When we look at someone with knowledge of certain imposed limiting factors, we tend to accept those limitations. Some people question this philosophy by asking, "How can you help if you don't know what's wrong?" Certainly teachers should learn all they can about a student, but I'm suggesting that, within reasonable parameters, we block out adult-imposed limitations. Believe in the student, and allow your compassion to help him through any difficulties.

I had a student who had trouble shifting his weight from one leg to the other. I began to work his independent muscle movement. I didn't know that for the first five years of his life he was unable to do this, and because I didn't impose that limiting belief,

within a few classes he was moving back and forth.
I think it would have taken me longer to get the
same results had I known about his limitation.

**A teacher affects eternity; he can never tell where
his influence stops.
—Henry B. Adams**

Another limiting belief prevalent in our society is
that children labeled with Attention Deficit Disorder
(ADD) or Attention Deficit Hyperactivity Disorder
(ADHD) have difficulty focusing. I know a coach
who believes all ADD/ADHD children are disruptive
and lack the ability to focus. He believes the only
way to overcome this is with the use of medication.
My guess is that he relies on medication rather than
his own teaching ability to focus that student.

I'm not suggesting that using a term like ADD or
ADHD is inappropriate to describe certain children's
behavior patterns. But if my student is not focusing,
it isn't his or her fault. If I believe that the child is at
fault, I may not work to my full potential. I might
accept that the medication is the only way for the
child to function and, in accepting those limitations,
fail to be the best teacher I can be.

There are many adult-imposed limitations on children in the world. I believe that teachers and coaches should be more inclined to look inward for the
answers instead of blaming the student, parents,
friends, or society as a whole. If you believe you
can't find the salt in the cabinet, you won't see it sitting on the shelf. If you believe the child can't do
something, you're probably right. If you believe he

can, he will.

Challenge

In 1990, I entered United States Air Force Undergraduate Pilot Training. The fourteen-hour days were grueling. I remember taking home flying manuals stacked over a foot high, absorbing the information before I fell asleep, then recalling it for a test the following day. Despite the hard work and "stress," it was one of the most enjoyable times of my life.

I was challenged.

Are your students challenged?

Give them challenges that are not arbitrary, but focused and directed at their own personal ability. Then watch them grow.

In grade school, I never won the Presidential Physical Fitness Award. I had the fifty-yard dash down. I was a master at the shuttle run. I was like a gazelle in the standing long jump. However, pull-ups gave me tremendous difficulty. I could only do two, but the requirement was six. That requirement so far exceeded my ability I was beaten before I started. Four pull-ups would have challenged me—six was just out of my reach.

As you allow yourself to care about each individual student, you will learn what the child can do easily and what challenges her. The greater the bond between teacher and child, the greater the potential for challenge.

During a proficiency test at the martial arts school in which students advance their belt color, I asked an instructor to hold the boards for each student to break. Jill was first, a six year old yellow belt testing for gold, all fifty pounds of her. Her uniform was about six inches too long and had to be safety-pinned to keep it from dragging on the floor. As Jill approached the board she glanced over to her mother. I couldn't tell if she even noticed the other seventy people sitting, waiting, wondering if this little brown-haired girl could possibly break a board. The instructor held the board steady as Jill stepped forward. She eyed the one inch pine, took a breath, and kicked. The board didn't break. The room fell silent, and I wished I could switch places with her. The instructor looked down and told her to "yell strong" as her foot hit. One more try...Jill stepped forward and yelled. Again her foot bounced off the board, this time reverberating her small body. The instructor looked down again and told her to "kick all the way through the board." Jill bit her lip and stepped forward, paused, and kicked a third time. Again no break. She burst into tears.

I knew Jill could break the board. She'd done it only two days earlier at a practice test. Sitting behind the judge's table, I looked at the students and parents all watching her. If she failed to break the board, we would have difficulty convincing her she was on a successful track. I moved from behind the table and caught Jill's eye, nodding in approval of her attempts. I took the board from the instructor and said, staring into her eyes, "You have the power and technique to break this board. We gave you that power—the same power you need to earn your black belt. The next step to black belt is to break this board with your foot. Yell strong and smash your foot completely through the wood. Do it now!"

Jill took a deep breath, stepped up and broke the board. The entire crowd cheered as I handed her the two boards that were once one. Without looking at me she grabbed the boards, wheeled around, and smiled at her mother.

Did breaking the boards challenge Jill? There was no question in my mind that she could break the boards. There might not have been doubt in Jill's mind either until her first miss. Caring and believing on the instructors' part is often all it takes to present a challenge that empowers students. Every child is different, and every challenge is different. If a teacher can present an insurmountable task as a possible accomplishment, over time the student will learn to do the same on her own. I had established a bond with Jill. That bond was necessary to pull her to new heights. I could get away with a great deal more "pushing" than any other instructor because the level of rapport was so great.

Reward

A teacher must reward a student at the completion of each step. The best rewards are tangible, something the student can see and put his hands on. The students earn rewards on several levels in our martial arts school. They first earn stripes around their belts, then eventually new colored belts. Some students even earn different colored uniforms. It's important that the reward be there for them to see and feel. And we see the results every day as the children carry around something they earned to show others. It becomes an anchor that triggers a certain emotional charge.

I first started awarding stripes on belts a few years ago. I asked Jack, a white belt taking his third class, to do a front kick. It was great. I brought him over to the side and awarded him with a piece of orange tape around his white belt. With great pride, he held his belt high all the way back to the line with the other students. The next day his parents told me how Jack placed his belt in his gym bag with the orange stripe sticking out and carried the bag to a birthday party to show everyone.

When is the right time to reward the student? When he does his best—not someone else's best, but *his* best. Caring and believing in the student is necessary to know if the challenge is appropriate. No two students will perform alike, because no two students are challenged alike.

"Appreciative words are the most powerful force for good on earth."
—George W. Crane

Praise

Praise goes beyond a pat on the back or an "attaboy." It is an intense moment between a student and a teacher that communicates complete approval. Praise encompasses all the Teaching Principles. It is the most important and the most difficult to master. It is also the most complex. In Chapter Six I discuss the ways to praise each and every student.

I will refer to these Teaching Principles often. They are the heart and soul of my empowering techniques.

DESIRED OUTCOME

To buy a car you must know what type, style, and

make you want. To pack for a trip you must know where you are going. To teach a class you must know what the students should learn. Know what you want for your students. Know why you are working with them. Visualize where they'll be in one year or ten years and what you want them to remember.

In my mind I have the desired outcome pictured vividly for each of my students. When I first opened my martial arts school, we trained our white belts hard. By the time they reached the first colored belt they were arguably the best yellow belts ever produced. The down side was that only two out of ten stayed past the third month. This was an obvious problem. I woke up one day and called a meeting with my instructors to re-identify our desired outcome.

What we wanted was not to have a student involved in the martial arts for one or two months, but to keep that student through black belt, a thirty-six month program. We re-worked our program and made changes in the rank requirements to keep our students longer, making good white belts into great black belts.

Keep in mind your desired outcome, and want more for each and every child. Want her to be so fundamentally sound that when she ventures out of your protective shelter, she makes decisions that will continue to empower her, leading her to new heights and opening greater opportunities for her to do whatever she wants, whenever she wants.

When someone asks what I want for my students, my response is to look at senior students, the ones who have been with me for over ten years. Mark is seventeen years old, a black belt, and a high school senior. His part-time job is teaching martial arts. He tells me that peer pressure is non-existent in his life.

Graybeal

He earns straight As and has a wonderful relationship with his parents and family. He earned various
scholarships to study mechanical engineering at a
prominent university and has success written all over
him. He excels at anything he does, from rock climbing to baseball. When I look at my students, I see
Mark as a well-rounded young adult with goals,
desires, and an attitude that is both cautious and
adventurous. I see the ideal desired outcome for all
of my students.

Chapter Three

What Happens
Inside Our Minds

"The greatest thing of the world is for a man to
know how to be his own."
—Michel de Montaigne

One Tuesday afternoon I walked into the martial arts school at 3:15. As usual, excitement
was beginning to fill the air. We were
expecting a new student, Franklin, for our three and
four year old "Tiny Tigers" class. Three mothers sat
in the back of the school. Another sat with her infant
son in our reception area. I didn't recognize her and
was about to introduce myself when I was called to
the office by one of my instructors. I noticed a little
confusion on the work-out floor, but class hadn't
started yet, and I thought that was the normal pre-
game unwind the students go through.

I turned at the sound of an instructor yelling,
"Franklin. Franklin!" A small brown-haired boy ran
around the floor aimlessly.

"Franklin, stop!" The instructor's voice began to
panic.

I saw Franklin's mother waving at her son. "You do what they tell you. Make sure you listen."

Let me first say that I do not allow any student to ignore the instructors because a martial arts school is a dangerous place not to listen. With that in mind I walked onto the floor and in my best commanding voice I erupted with one command. "FRANKLIN, STOP!!!"

Needless to say everyone else stopped too, including all the students, instructors, and parents waiting for their classes to begin. Franklin stopped and looked up at me. I lowered myself down to his eye level, introduced myself, and told him that what he was doing was not okay.

Now I'm not suggesting that we all walk around yelling at children. What I am suggesting is that we have a clear understanding of how to interact with them. Why were the other teachers unable to get control of Franklin? We talked about that after class, and most said they didn't want to offend the mother, so they let the child walk all over them. It is essential to have the ability to gain control of any situation. For the safety and well-being of your students, the need to do what is right should never be compromised.

INTERNAL AND EXTERNAL COMMUNICATION

We all remember speech class and discussing the process of communication. We learned the technical side of how to outline our thoughts and structure speeches. But did we really learn it all? Years ago I discovered a book by Michael Brooks based on Neurolinguistic-Programming or NLP. His book,

Instant Rapport, broke down the communication process into language I could understand. It explained why and how certain words trigger certain responses. He went on to suggest how to establish a bond while communicating. It was my first phase in understanding that what people say and what people mean are sometimes two distinctly different things. What you say is less important than what the other person hears and understands.

The Internal Voice

When I first tried to understand communication, I concentrated on the external—things I said and how I said them to other people. I felt that what was happening in my own mind was fine; my goal was to increase the level of understanding in my listener's mind. I attended seminar after seminar and read book after book, hearing the same thing—internal communication was just as important as external communication. I set a goal to understand internal communication completely.

Internal communication is what makes up who you are. It is that voice inside your mind that tells you to run a mile or eat a piece of cake. It tells you if you are happy or sad. It tells you if you like your job or hate it. Think of the possibilities that could come from commanding your internal voice. Think of the possibilities that could come from instilling quality internal communication in your students. That internal voice will tell children to study or to watch television. It will tell them to give to charity or to steal a candy bar. It will tell them they are happy or tell them they are sad.

I can't directly control the internal communication of children, but I can teach them skills that are structured and focused, that will allow them to create a compelling future, and will empower their internal communication. Once we master these skills, success is inevitable.

The External Voice

In the early 1970's, Professor Albert Mehrabian of UCLA concluded that people communicate in three primary ways—the words we use, the voice inflection or tonalities that we bring to those words, and our body language or physiology. According to his research, physiology accounts for 55 percent of external communication, tonalities or voice inflection account for 38 percent, and the specific words we use account for about seven percent.

Body language is the visual side of communication. It's the most important of the three and the easiest to adjust. It, in turn, affects the other communication aspects. Chapters Six and Seven contain several ways to increase your communication skills with the use of body language.

A teacher must have a wide range of voice inflections to convey a broad range of ideas. Have you ever heard someone say, "It's not what you said, it's how you said it?" When I was growing up, people would often tell me how dramatic I was. Now, I put my dramatics to use every time I work with a child by sharing with him my multiple characters and multiple voices.

Several years ago while at a conference in Palm Springs, I spoke with one of my many mentors in the martial arts. He was unsurpassed in his ability to enroll students in his school, and I asked him what he said to prospective students that made the difference. I pulled up a chair, turned on a tape recorder, and suggested we begin a role-playing exercise. "I'll be one of your future students at an enrollment conference. I want to hear everything." My intention was to make a script for myself and my instructors.

"It's not what you say that's important," he answered. "Most people are looking for the words. But remember, the specific words only account for seven percent of communication."

I insisted. He obliged, and I wrote a script. I then tried to put it to use. In an ever-changing environment where people can ask many different questions, it just didn't work. Though the preparation helped me with the other parts of communication, the script couldn't convey the passion I have for martial arts.

Have some fun with this. Vary your body language, your voice inflections, and your facial expressions. Watch the impact your "message" gives your student.

How you place words together will elicit different pictures, sounds, and feelings in the minds of your listeners. Many books discuss the way we communicate. My favorite is the _Structure of Magic_ by Richard Bandler and John Grindler. This book looks at specific word patterns and which parts of the brain we activate with their use.

THE CODES

I like to refer to our five senses as *codes*. We can hear sounds (auditory), have feelings (kinesthetic), see pictures (visual), smell (olfactory), and taste (gustatory). A good communicator will access all these codes. Think of our minds as computers with floppy disk drives. The information we have stored on disks that go into our floppy drives contains programs that include binary codes for each of the five senses. (In computer lingo binary means either on or off.) For each revolution of the disk there are five tracks of information, and each code or sense has its own track. When information is saved on a disk, at least one track must be used (i.e. sounds, feelings, pictures, smells, or tastes.) Think of a memory you have of something that happened last week. The entire memory only contains a combination of five senses. It is something you saw, heard, tasted, smelled, or felt and nothing more.

The goal of a teacher should be to save information on the students' disks using at least three of the tracks. Most likely the three options are auditory, kinesthetic, and visual.

If a teacher instructs by accessing auditory inputs only, the student will be left starved for more information. The teacher used just one track or twenty percent of the available input. Could this be why children's minds wander?

Children use their codes differently. They have not yet learned to analyze, sort, and discard input that seems unimportant, as we adults do.

At a children's class one morning, I watched five year old Jennifer sniff the boy standing next to her. I stopped and watched in amazement as this little girl smelled her friend's face.

"What are you doing?"

"Sniffing Michael," she said, smiling ear to ear.

I just smiled back, searching for a response and finding none.

In addition to what I mentioned earlier, everyone communicates differently. Some people like to hear sounds, others like to see pictures, and still others are looking for the right feeling.

I had a professor in college who was strictly an auditory communicator. One day he was with a hearing impaired student and the student's interpreter. The student was having difficulty turning his work in on time, and the frustration was apparent in the professor's voice. Repeatedly he asked, "Do you hear what I'm saying?"

Everyone responds differently to the available inputs. As teachers, we must focus on how the student communicates and learns best and not solely on how we like to communicate.

These codes are programmed on our disks from the first day we enter the world, and every experience is saved containing at least one of the five senses. Often the most memorable programs stored are the ones that contain all five. As teachers, we must investigate and remember how each of our students prefer to learn and which of the inputs maximize learning. Then use those inputs when we teach to store information on the student's disks.

THE CODES AND TEACHING

One of my own martial arts teachers once told me there are three ways to teach someone—tell them, show them, and touch them. Just as certain people like certain types of music—some people like the blues, some like jazz, still others like classical music—your students will respond differently to certian inputs. Some like to learn by feeling, by listening, or seeing. Our job is to find out what type of "music" they like and then interlink that music with the information we want the student to have.

If a student likes the blues and you constantly play classical music, will she learn effectively? Or will she simply hear the beat and never quite experience or remember the entire song? If a student responds to visual teaching but you teach through touch, how effectively will she learn? Can a blues lover learn to listen to classical music? Sure, but will he enjoy it as much as the blues? A visual student can learn from teachers using kinesthetic codes, but that student will not learn as fast or be as productive.

Let's look at three students—Gina, Laurie, and Stephanie. Each student learns differently. Gina always looks up. She moves her hands in an animated fashion. She always wants to see what's happening. She often uses sight words like see, picture, clear, etc. when she talks to her teacher. She is visual. A teacher might show her how to tie her shoes by tying her own shoes.

Laurie always wants to hear more. She likes to hear stories. She is auditory. A teacher might talk her through tying her shoes.

Stephanie walks with her head down and does not say much. She always hugs her teacher before and after class. She uses feeling words like touch, grasp, hold, etc. She is kinesthetic. Her teacher might help her fingers with the laces.

With a conscious effort, teachers can begin to pick up how each student learns. A large class should encompass all learning styles. And don't forget the last two—taste and smell. Teachers can use such phrases as, "You are so close you can taste it," or "You can smell victory."

Remember how your students learn.

When is the last time you heard someone say they could remember a face but not a name? As a teacher, remembering who you're talking to is crucial. _Mega Memory_ by Kevin Trudeau can take you through a simple process that teaches you how to link names to faces. I see more than two hundred students each week, and I'm able to remember each one. I can tell you their parents' names, dogs' names, and where they go to school. Most importantly, I remember how they prefer to learn. If a student learns best with her eyes, I picture that student with large eyes. If the student learns best with his ears, I picture him with elephant ears. If that student learns best by touching, I picture her with spiders crawling across her body. It sounds strange, I know, but sometimes linking a vivid or strange picture will lock the data into your own memory bank.

THE TWO PARTS OF THE MIND

Let's separate the mind into two components—conscious and unconscious. By understanding how these two parts interact, we can understand how to empower our students effectively.

The Conscious Mind

In 1956, George Miller determined that the conscious mind is capable of having seven, plus or minus two, thoughts at any one time. Our unconscious mind stores all other thoughts or information.

Think of your phone number or the first car you owned. That information was locked somewhere in your unconscious mind. You opened a file cabinet, removed a floppy disk, and placed it into one of your floppy drives, your conscious mind. When you did this, some other disk most likely shifted back to your unconscious. Do you remember what it was?

Picture the conscious mind as nine "floppy drives" ready for action and the unconscious mind as the storage system for your floppy disks. The key to focused learning is to get only one drive working at a time while the other drives are idle.

The Unconscious Mind

For our purposes, let's call the unconscious mind the storage system for our disks. Saved on our disks is everything we have ever seen, smelled, heard, tasted, and felt. The storage system is massive and makes up who we are. These floppy disks are also linked together, and sometimes, if you access a disk, other disks may follow into one of the other drives. (We call this an anchor.) Our internal communication comes from the information on those disks. To make our students successful, we want to ensure that we give them quality information to store.

MAKING DECISIONS

Remember the story about Andrew, the young black belt who stopped at the traffic accident? Why did he stop and rush to help? How does a child learn to make empowered decisions?

Children's lives revolve to a large extent around how well they can manipulate their bodies. Think back to grade school. Remember when the two sides picked teams? I remember as if it were yesterday.

How devastating it was to run across the gym floor, the last one chosen. It wasn't very empowering, yet children go through this every day. We can't make every child a star athlete, but we can learn to empower them on their own level. We can empower them through the Teaching Principles. We can take time to understand how to teach, how children make decisions, and how their internal communication fits into their decision-making process.

Children make decisions based on how they feel about themselves. How they feel about themselves is based on the compelling future they create in their minds. The compelling future is based on their internal communication.

While I was writing this book, a DARE officer from the local police department gave a talk on how to "say no to drugs." Robby, a twelve year old blue belt, commented that an older boy had recently offered him drugs after school. He said no. What provided the basis for his decision?

I have seen children make both desirable and undesirable choices, and the children who make desirable choices are those who feel good about themselves. They have at least one aspect in their life that is empowering.

Let's analyze what might have been happening inside Robby. He is not the best all-around athlete and he knows what it's like to be picked last for a team. (I never allow children to pick teams for this reason. In my school the instructors always assign teams.) But each time Robby leaves his martial arts lesson, he feels good about what he can do because we're working at his level. He also feels that someone cares about teaching him. He feels he is good at something because the instructors convey that to him during every class. Robby is learning to create quality internal communication. He continues to listen to his internal voice, the one that tells him he's important, the one that tells him that no matter what happens he's good at something and has an exciting future. No matter how mean others are to him, he still has his parents, teacher, and martial arts instructor who care. With powerful internal communication do you think he would use drugs?

Children are bombarded through television, relationships, games, teachers, friends, and siblings. It's our responsibility as teachers and coaches to save only high-quality information on their disks, information that will allow them to ask better questions, get better answers, and make better decisions.

Once we empower children with positive internal communication, their decision-making process becomes successful. Take a child and teach her something, something she wants to learn. Teach her something that will give her an edge, something that attacks all of the inputs, something that can become part of her. Let it contain a physical action, an auditory input, and a visual stimulus. Let it fill up her disks. Let it empower her mind.

"Success...seems to be connected with action.
Successful people keep moving. They make mistakes, but they don't quit."
—Conrad Hilton

There are many components to enhancing children, and teachers must use all the possible inputs. Since so many children are kinesthetic or visual, we must understand the importance of conveying a feeling through the visual stimulus we communicate to them. We need to have a better understanding of how children make choices that enable and empower them to make a positive impact.

Chapter Four

What Fails Children

"The past is of no importance. The present is of no importance. It is with the future that we have to deal."
—Oscar Wilde

"If you don't stop that you're gonna have another thing coming!"

"If your friend jumped off a bridge would you jump off too?"

"Don't make me stop this car!"

"Is there something you would like to share with the class?"

You've heard them all—comments that did nothing but confuse, or worse, compound the situation. In this chapter we'll analyze what we say and why certain words are damaging.

SELF-FULFILLING PROPHECIES

I greeted a prospective new member to my martial arts school the other day. The dad, 35, the eight year old son, and the seven year old daughter, all sat down to learn about our school. I asked a few questions and sat in amazement at the response. The father began to tell me about his son who was "shy, not athletic, and not very good at school." With each statement, I watched the son sink lower and lower into the chair. Right before my very eyes this dad was destroying his son. I quickly changed the subject.

As I mentioned in the section on Belief, students often become what we believe they will become. I recently visited with a parent who told me her child was unruly, could not sit still in class, and would be up running around in a matter of seconds.

If a teacher believes a child will be unruly, chances are he will be. I impose no limiting beliefs on my students and expect model behavior from each one.

Limiting beliefs become part of a child's makeup. Do you ever talk with a child at an activity, a soccer game or a recital, and ask, "Are you nervous?" Do you ever introduce a child as "hyperactive?" Do you ever introduce a child as having "ADD" or learning disabilities? Children pick up on everything you say about them and save those words on their disks. It's our job as adults to only let empowering information enter their minds.

I remember hearing a story about a father who had three sons. He introduced them like this, "This is my oldest son, Billy. He's the genius of the family. This is my middle son, Jimmy. He's the athlete of the family. This is my third son, Eddy. He's a little shy."

One afternoon the father pondered the manner in which he introduced his children and decided to try an experiment. The next time he introduced his children he said, "This is my oldest son, Billy. He's a super student. This is Jimmy, an outstanding athlete.

And this is Eddy. He's very outgoing." Eddy began to change and evolve into the person described in his father's introduction. Prophecies hold true.

"The most important thing about goals is having one."
—Geoffrey F. Abert

RESPONSIBILITY

When we talk about what fails children, there is a simple response.

Adults fail children.

Lack of responsibility from adults is a recurring theme that can sum up a great many problems. I want a society that is empowered. I want a society where crime is non-existent. I want a society that affords all people the chance for success. Am I an idealist? Sure. If we all felt this way, if we all worked with every child we contact, if we all took responsibility, think of the possibilities.

Is there a gap?

Parents take responsibility when a child is with them, although we all know that an increasing number of children do not spend the majority of their time at home. Sometimes schoolteachers take on an ever-increasing role since some children spend more time with the schoolteacher than anyone else. There are three major players in our Support Triangle—parent, schoolteacher, and martial arts instructor. Sometimes there may be a gap in responsibility, leaving the child unprotected. When adults shift responsibility to others, which happens frequently, disastrous results often follow.

Visiting with a parent one afternoon, I contemplated this. What if the teacher at school took complete responsibility for everything that happened in the child's life from the time he rose in the morning until he fell asleep, including time at home, at school, and with friends? What would happen if the parent also took complete responsibility? And if the martial arts teacher did the same?

I was listening to a radio talk show the other day and a husband and wife were having marital problems. The wife said the husband was not always honest with her. The husband agreed and said, "I learned how to be dishonest from my parents."

What an *awful* trait to instill in your children!

But was he taking responsibility for lying? Most people would agree that we shouldn't blame others for our actions, but I think we need to take it a step further. I'm completely responsible for each and every child who enters my school. I cannot relinquish that responsibility to someone else. My responsibility to the child includes empowering him to take responsibility for his actions while he is in martial arts school and out. Helping him do this is one of the best ways for him to learn. I am the one who accepted responsibility, and I must answer for that decision while he is under my supervision.

The day we take responsibility for everything in our lives is the day we say goodbye to failure and latch onto success. When we teach our students to take personal responsibility, we empower them.

A martial arts instructor whom I know recently had his house vandalized. He later learned the extensive damage was done by his neighbor's son, a seventeen year old named Chris. After Chris's arrest, his attorney contacted my friend who offered a suggestion. Instead of Chris's mother paying the insurance deductible, Chris would work it off by painting my friend's house. In addition, Chris would become a member of the martial arts school for a minimum of one year. My friend wanted nothing more than to work with this young man and personally empower him toward a successful future through responsibility.

NEGATIVE WORDS

Remember that the disk storage system which makes up our unconscious mind in essence represents who we are. When a teacher tells a child he's "bad" she attacks the disk storage system, the main part of who he is. I can't stress enough the need to only attack what is *playing on the disk*, the specific act or behavior the child is engaged in, and not the storage system itself. The act or information on the disk is often mistakenly attacked by teachers, leading to disastrous results. Use caution when you reprimand a child. Understand that they are what you have helped create. They are responding to you and to the environment you have established, and negative words that are not thought out disempower children.

SUPPORT

If a teacher or coach strays away from supporting the triangle, the ability to teach the student will diminish. As a child, it was clear to me that my parents completely supported my teacher. Consequently, my behavior at school was relatively successful because I knew my parents were one hundred percent behind my teachers. In the Support

Triangle one hundred percent support from the parents, teachers, and instructors can launch students to heights never before experienced. As a member of the Support Triangle, I must show complete support when something happens on another side. The details can be investigated outside the presence of the child. Nevertheless, we must support that person if we are going to maximize the benefit we give that student.

Christopher, a student of mine for over two years, was having trouble listening at school. He was twelve years old and a joy to have in my class. His parents and I talked about his problem, and I asked if it was okay for me to visit with the teacher. The next day I set up a meeting, and while visiting with his teacher it was apparent she was not a "people person." During our visit four students asked her a question, and while she did respond, the answers were short and uncaring. In my opinion she didn't enjoy teaching, and I'm sure if she were my teacher I would have had trouble too. However, though I was sympathetic to Christopher's situation, I had to show him I supported his teacher. If I didn't, the respect she needed to teach would dissolve even further.

I spent time with Christopher and reinforced the respect he needed to give to his teacher. I explained that throughout life he would have to work with people who might not be his favorite, but that he'd have to learn to make the best of it.

PUNISHMENT

Adults use several terms for correcting a student. Some call it discipline, and some call it punishment. Some use the term penalty. I'll term anything that causes pain, loss, or suffering to a student as punishment. Punishment should be inflicted only in order to persuade him not to do an undesirable act again.

Far too often, adults instruct a student to sit in a corner or perform some task without telling him why. "Think about what you just did and come back when you are sorry." Does that sound familiar? When a teacher punishes a student, it's crucial that the student understands what is happening and why. You can simply explain, "When you do this, I feel like this, because of this." It's a time for communication and understanding, not silence. An instructor may say to a student, "When I'm speaking and you are talking in class, I feel bad because it causes me to lose focus. Therefore, I'm not the best teacher I can be. Because you were talking after I asked you not to, I want you to move off to the side of the floor and wait until this drill is over as punishment."

Explain how you feel, then ask the child to repeat it back and describe what he should have done. Listen and make sure he understands why he received the correction. Then practice the scenario again to verify that he understands the correct action.

The other day in class I saw a young man lose control of his legs. He stood there and, without external forces (or at least any I could see), collapsed to the ground, rocking back and forth like a sixty pound tortoise on his back. I looked across the floor and wondered exactly what was happening. He hopped back up. When the instructor turned to another student, the boy lost complete control again.

I know what it's like to hold a large amount of energy inside because I'm about as hyperactive as they come. However, flopping around on the floor is not acceptable at my school. I commanded the young man to have a seat.

"Do you know why you aren't participating in class?"

"Nope." He answered.

"You decided to flop around on the floor like a tortoise, and that is not okay. So you have to sit out as punishment."

"Yes, sir."

"Do you know why you are sitting out of class?"

"Because I wasn't standing like I was supposed to."

"Very good. Do you know what punishment is?" I asked.

"No." He answered.

I then took the time to tell him what punishment means and reminded him that his behavior was not acceptable. That was the last time I had to discipline that student because I took the time to make sure he knew what was happening. You can avoid many painful struggles if you communicate.

IS THAT PUNISHMENT?

With these guidelines in mind, let's take a closer look at punishment. First, for punishment to be punishment, it must have a negative consequence for the child. That is, it should be unacceptable to the child.

Years ago, one of my students was causing a problem in class. When I first started teaching martial arts, we sometimes had students do push-ups for punishment. We thought push-ups would cause the student's shoulders to become sore and persuade the individual not to repeat whatever resulted in his having to do the push-ups in the first place.

This particular student was a small five year old boy who couldn't really perform push-ups. Instead,

I instructed him to stand with his arms held straight out. His mother came in the following day and asked to speak with me.

"You know, that was really an unacceptable form of punishment. He was so horrified and embarrassed about what happened he wouldn't even tell me why he had to stand with his arms out. It's perfectly fine to have him sit down and give him a time-out. You can give him a time-out for as long as you want; do it for the entire class period if necessary."

If it's acceptable to the student, is anything learned?

A police officer told me once about a street gang that requires members to go to prison. It wasn't important what they did, just as long as they served time "to toughen them up." Is prison acceptable to those gang members? Yes. Then is prison a viable form of punishment for them?

If sitting in a chair in a time-out is acceptable for a child and a teacher uses sitting in a chair as punishment, then it is not true punishment. If not watching TV is acceptable and TV privileges are removed, is it punishment? It is important that we find things that are unacceptable to a child, otherwise it is an exercise in futility. What is unacceptable? That depends on the child. If the punishment is unacceptable then that behavior should subside. If the behavior doesn't change, chances are the punishment is not working, and in the child's mind it is acceptable.

I visited a martial arts school in New Jersey one afternoon. A young student named Tony was in an energetic mood. Five minutes before class he kicked the bottled-water dispenser in the back room and the instructor sent him out on the floor to do 1,000 front kicks as punishment. How do you think Tony felt towards front kicks after that? Do not make the punishment something you want the child to learn to enjoy. Teachers must determine if punishment is appropriate for a student's action and to what degree. The best way for a teacher or coach to deter a student from repeating a known undesirable action is through quick, immediate, undesirable, yet appropriate punishment. I call this reformatting the disk. When a child begins to play a disk with less than desirable tracks, the teacher must interrupt what is playing, reformat the disk, and lay down better information. Otherwise the action will repeat itself.

"In order to succeed, you must know what you are doing, like what you are doing, and believe in what you are doing."
—Will Rogers

THE ANSWERS WE GIVE

During my childhood, I remember getting answers that I didn't understand. It drove me crazy when my mother or father would say, "No, just because."

I would ask, "Can I go to the park?"

"No."

"Why not?"

"Well, just because."

I had written on one of my disks that questioning directives from adults was okay. In our martial arts class when an instructor answers a student, the student is not allowed to question that answer. Of course, I'm referring only to directive answers and not answers given while teaching.

For example, if a student asks, "Can I get a drink

of water?" And the instructor answers, "No," the student is not allowed to question that directive. The information, or binary code, we saved on her disks does not permit that type of question. This is an element of respect and discipline which leads to a powerful learning environment.

But we never respond with just a "No."

Instead, we tell the student why.

"Mr. Graybeal, can I break a board?"

"No." I pause for him to accept the answer and insure he doesn't question it, then continue, "We only have a certain number of boards in the school," or "We don't have time for that today because we are beginning the next class."

I give the student real reasons.

Students understand and are able to appreciate my answer. It takes a great deal of discipline to accept answers from teachers in such a manner, but this type of discipline empowers children because it leads to a focused, not a wandering mind.

COMMUNICATION LEVELS

Children most often look up to see the person teaching them. When communicating with a shorter student, a good teacher must use eye level contact to her advantage. While looking up you enter a visual state. While looking down you enter a kinesthetic state. When physically looking up you distance yourself from that person. I read a newspaper article the other day that said the taller presidential candidate is more likely to win the election. If you want your students to look up to you, have them look up. If you want the students to enter a level of communication where they are open, have them look down. By looking down they enter a kinesthetic state and open up their feelings.

Teachers can establish a level of caring the first time they meet a student by lowering themselves to the child's eye level. People like people that are like them. If I'm working with a child and I'm really trying to get him to open up, I have him sit in a chair and I sit on the floor. He gets to look down to someone, something he's not done his entire day. Try it, it works.

QUALITY TIME

I'm a big believer in quality time, not quantity time. I think it only takes one to two seconds to enjoy quality time with a child. Our martial arts classes are 45 minutes long, and we might have twenty students in a class. There are many one to two second time blocks in a 45 minute period—opportunities for the instructor to have quality time with each child in every class.

What three components do you need for quality time? You need an auditory stimulus, a visual stimulus, and a kinesthetic stimulus. Drop down to the child's eye level. Touch him on the shoulder or the arm, and let that become an anchor, the same place you'll always touch him while praising. Give him a special look, a thumbs-up, and overlap that by telling him specifically how well he's doing. For example, "Your focus today, Johnny, was the best focus I have ever seen you deliver in class. You know what? I'm proud of you. With focus like this, you'll be a super black belt."

UNDERSTANDING

While teaching a beginning class I asked a young boy, Danny, to lift his leg to his chest. He lifted it to his waist. I then asked again, "Lift your knee up to your chest. Do you understand?"

He answered, "Yes, sir," and lifted his leg waist height. The child said he understood but still failed to do what I asked. Did he really understand?

I dropped down on my knees. "Do you know where your knee is?"

"Yes sir."

Then I asked if he knew where his chest was.

"Yes, sir."

I stood up and waited. Again, the knee did not come up above the waist. I asked, "Do you understand what I want you to do?" The student answered with a yes, but by this time it was apparent he did not. With that I started all over. I showed him what to do then told him what to do. I finally picked his leg up and moved it throughout the proper range of motion. Finally he understood.

Students must have a clear understanding of what the teacher wants. After you tell a child something or teach a child something, have him repeat it back. For example, "Do you understand why it's important for you to say, 'Yes, sir,' when I give you a directive?" If the child responds with, "Because you told me so," I did not communicate effectively. I explain to her that when she responds with, "Yes, sir," it lets me know she heard what I said.

If you become frustrated with a student who doesn't understand, both you and the student lose. If you become compassionate and understanding, you both win.

CONSISTENCY

Consistency is the most confusing element in teacher/student relationships. You must be honest and courteous, and you must follow through to the end. When you give a directive you MUST hold true to it. Murphy's Law promises that the student is always going to remember an inconsistency, even if it only happens a few times.

Inconsistency leads to an increased distance. Remember the first Teaching Principle: Caring. You must care about the child enough to be consistent, honest, and demonstrate a high level of integrity. The child only knows what is saved on his disks, and everything that happens in his life will be etched there forever. If we repeat something often enough, the grooves become so deep that reformatting becomes difficult. Etch only quality information.

Chapter Five

Points to Ponder

"Your past is important, but it is not nearly as important to your present as is the way you see your future."
—Dr. Tony Campolo

LIMITED INPUTS FOR CORRECTING

There are several available inputs teachers or coaches can use to communicate with their students. Understanding how to use them for productive teaching is essential. If a student needs correcting, take him aside and choose one of the three inputs: kinesthetic, auditory, or visual, but never overlap all three. Save that for praising. Remind the student what happened. Often children forget or don't know what they did and why it's not acceptable. Ask the student what a better decision might have been. This will give him tools to become successful and techniques that will lead him forward.

Often I will only whisper a correction into a child's ear, turning my face away so he cannot see me. At the end of that brief correction, the praise begins. I step back, look the child in his eyes, and again tell him that his behavior was not like him. I ask the child to repeat what I said and why that type of behavior is unacceptable. I then praise him specifically for listening while touching him on the shoulder. I tell him how proud I am he had a chance to learn from this experience and I trust that it won't happen again. This leaves the student understanding the correction and avoids bad feelings toward the teacher or himself.

SELF-CRITIQUING

Some refer to it as "natural consequences." I term it "self-critiquing." This is perhaps one of the best ways for a child to learn. If you are running with your shoes untied and fall, chances are you're going to start tying your shoe laces. If you forget your coat, go outside, and get cold, chances are you are not going to forget it again.

Teachers avoid badgering the child when they allow children to learn through self-critiquing, though it goes without saying that teachers must closely monitor these experiences to insure a high level of safety.

THE "IF-THEN" STATEMENT

Several linguistic patterns or words are detrimental to the successful empowerment of children. We'll start with the dreaded "if-then statement."

"If you finish your dinner, then you'll get an ice cream cone."

"If you don't clean up your things, then you will have to sit out."

Several times a week I hear adults say to children "if something, then this." I would speculate that the adult follows through only a small percentage of the time. The "if-then statement" sets everyone up for failure time and time again.

One afternoon a mother and I were discussing some of the problems adults have communicating with children, using word patterns like the "if-then" statement. She explained how once she said to her daughter, "If you don't bring your grades up, then you're not going to the Madonna concert."

The daughter didn't bring her grades up, but the mother had spent a considerable amount of time acquiring the Madonna tickets, so the daughter went anyway. The next week over dinner her son brought it up, "I thought you said that if she didn't get better grades, then she couldn't go to the concert."

It's not the use of consequences that is detrimental. It's the use of the "if-then" word pattern that fires a button inside the minds of our students that is the problem. That button sends a disk into the drive that reminds the student that "if-then" does not mean much. Therefore, the student doesn't listen, and the teacher has set herself up for failure.

If a teacher explains to a student exactly what the consequences are for a given behavior and the student does not obey, *then* the teacher *must* follow through by imposing those consequences.

The "if-then" statement also finds its way into a reward, thus becoming a bribe. We all know that life is an "if-then" statement. If you eat, then you won't be hungry. If you clean your room, then you'll be able to find your clothes. If you exercise, then you'll be in good shape. "If you continue to practice your new kicks each day, then I'll give you a special 'kicker' patch for your uniform." That statement is an official bribe. Rewarding students should only happen after they've done their best. "You are now promoted to black belt in recognition of your dedication, perseverance, and spirit involved in your training."

I sat in the office one afternoon as a young instructor was playing around with some students before the next class. There were seven four year olds running around the floor, enjoying themselves immensely. As class time approached, he told them to lineup. They ignored him. In desperation, he turned to an old faithful, if-then-statement. "If you don't line up right now, then we're not going to have class." These young children were only four, but even at that young age they knew when the adult didn't mean what he said. Could the young instructor have used a more productive word pattern? Yes, simply by restructuring the words, avoiding the "if-then" statement. Instead of using "if you don't line up for class now then we won't have class," the instructor could say, "Line up now for class," without giving consequences. If the students don't line up, the appropriate disciplinary action should be taken. "Class will be canceled due to the students not lining up." The point to remember is to avoid the combination of the "if-then" words without appropriate, enforceable consequences.

THINK ABOUT THAT

The next unsuccessful linguistic pattern I often hear is, "Go stand over there while you think about what you just did." Rampant confusion ensues in the child's mind. When there is a slip, a mistake, an unsuccessful trait that leaks out from one of our students, we need to take responsibility. Great teachers instill skills in their students, while statements like "think about it" do nothing to address what happened. If you see an unsuccessful behavior pattern emerging, be specific and detailed about it. For example, "Yesterday I was unhappy with the amount of time you practiced your martial arts. Instead of ten minutes, today I would like to see you work for fifteen." Or, "I am having you sit down as punishment for not following directions." With follow-up questions, you can be certain the child knows what is happening. "Did you know what the directions were?" Students only know what we, their teachers, program on their disks.

A THREE-LETTER WORD

The word "but" is extremely damaging to the communication process. "That was a great front kick, **but** it would be a better front kick if you'd get your knee higher."

How does that student feel? What did we communicate? Does he really think he has a good kick? Instead, I say, "That's a great front kick, and you know what? It will be an even better front kick once you bring your knee higher." Or, "Hey, those are great grades, and you know what? You'll have even better grades next time by studying for thirty minutes each night."

I will only use a "but" statement when I want to nullify what was said first. For example, I will ask a child, "Do you know what part of the foot makes contact when throwing a side kick?"

If the child says, "I don't know," I will respond

with, "I know you don't know, **but** if you did know, what would you say?" The "but" statement (question) gives the child the opportunity to say what he or she *does* know, without having to live up to some perceived expectation that the student knows the whole answer.

Words really mean something. However, some of the words we use do little to communicate what we want to say.

DAMAGING PATTERNS

Another damaging pattern is when we compare one child to another. I never turn to a student and say, "I would never expect your brother to act like that. What's going through your mind?"

Teachers need to allow each student to be an individual and each child to understand that he or she is special. Teachers should hold children to their individual standards and remember that a child is only challenged by doing his or her best, not his or her brother's or sister's best. Let the child know you care about what he can do, then step out of the way, and let it happen.

GUESSING

Children are often reluctant to give answers, even to the point of shutting down. We must allow the child to understand that guessing is okay. Tell a quick story about guessing: "I once guessed at an answer and got it right," or, "I once guessed at the lottery and won." Once a child understands that speaking her mind is okay, we have the chance to establish a strong foundation for communicating and sharing information. By doing this, I hope to encourage students to sit in the classroom and answer more questions when asked. At archery camp, they will be able to raise their hands and ask the proper way to draw on the target. When they become confused with life, they will go to their mentors and ask questions about important issues.

ANSWER THAT QUESTION

Why do we as teachers ask questions? The reasons I ask my students questions is to see if I'm connecting with them. In other words, I'm checking myself to see if I'm being effective.

Last fall I took a few classes at the local university and in the second week the professor began to ask questions. Being one to talk a lot, I raised my hand and attempted to answer a simple question about how Sulfur and Oxygen combine to form Sulfur (IV) Oxide. I answered incorrectly. The eighteen year old sitting next to me didn't. To my total bewilderment, he answered correctly. I felt pretty stupid. On the way home it dawned on me. In my classes when a student answers incorrectly, I either help that student remember or give him the answer. Rarely do I call on someone else to answer the same question. As a result, if a student answers a question incorrectly, he doesn't give up. He simply moves on, undeterred by the subject or teacher.

DRAMATIC AND EMOTIONAL

Humans learn best and remember most when an

event is emotional and dramatic. I look for such opportunities with my students.

When I was in third grade, a kid on my bus, Greg, brought fireworks to school. He showed them to everyone. They were the small "lady finger" type. He kept them a secret all day until he was about to burst. Finally he spilled the beans and asked if anybody wanted them. Sharing some of Greg's excitement, I took a few home and showed them to my dad. The next day everyone in the school knew about the fireworks, and I soon learned that fireworks were not allowed in school. My teacher asked about them and prepared me for a trip to the principal's office. I was in terror. For the next hour I sat in my chair, allowing my mind to conjure up all the unpleasant things the principal was going to do to me. At exactly 10:00 a.m. I heard my name crackle over the loud speaker with instructions to report to the principal's office. My heart stopped, and I sank into my chair hoping no one would notice me. Greg joined me in the dark hallway as we began the long journey toward the office of doom. I was first to enter.

The principal asked if I knew about the fireworks. My hands began to sweat, and I tried again to hide in the large orange plastic interrogation chair. "Yes sir. I took them home, and my father and I tried to light them off, but they didn't work." I hoped their inability to ignite would lessen the infraction.

He responded by telling me how dangerous they were and said it was against school rules to have them on the bus. Then he said, "Thank you for being honest. Go sit outside."

I wasn't sure if I was out of the woods yet, but I knew I was honest, and that was most important. At least that was what my parents told me, and at eight years of age I was inclined to believe them.

Next, the principal asked Greg into his office. I listened as Greg concocted a wonderful story. It was sheer brilliance as he told of two older boys, the police, and a robbery. He ended the story by telling the principal that he had last seen the fireworks on the other side of the fence, off school property.

"Brilliant," I said to myself, sure I had made a mistake. My impassioned speech rooted in honesty had failed me. What was I doing listening to my parents? I should have gone with my gut instincts. I was a man of the world. I could have told a great story.

The principal poked his head outside the office and looked at me. I took a deep breath and waited. "Go back to your class," was all he said.

Nothing happened to me because I was honest. Greg received harsh punishment, and for the rest of the day he walked back and forth circling the fence searching for the mysterious "lady fingers."

That was such an emotional event for me that it is still vivid in my mind. I have been honest ever since, in part because of one dramatic event in the principal's office which supported what my parents had taught me.

The other day in the martial arts school a senior-student told me that a child had kicked one of the restroom doors. I asked which student, and he pointed him out.

I called Zachary into the conference room. I sat down in a chair. The young man started to sit also and I firmly reminded him that he was to stand at attention and await my questioning.

"Explain what happened in the rest room."

"Well, this other boy, John, he kicked the door."

"Are you sure you didn't kick the door?"

"No." he said turning away and looking down.

I asked John to step into the room, alone, and I asked him what happened. He said, "Zachary kicked the door."

I brought both boys back in. "Which one kicked the door?"

At exactly the same time, they pointed to each other.

"One of you is being dishonest, and dishonesty is not a trait that is acceptable in our martial arts school. To become a black belt and to become successful, we first must have honesty in our hearts."

I left to investigate and spoke with one of the other instructors. He told me what he had seen. Armed with this ammunition, I returned to speak with Zachary, still standing at attention. I informed him that one of our black belts saw what happened.

"Well, I kind of just touched the door with my foot. But the other kid, he was the one who kicked it closed." His eyes went down, and he entered what appeared to be a completely remorseful state. At that point I changed my own physiology, my facial expressions and my voice, from stern to proud. I pulled up a chair and I asked him to sit.

"I'm very proud of you Zachary. Can I tell you a story?"

I told him the firecracker story. "Remember that it's never too late to be honest. It's never too late to bring the entire story out, and because of that, I'm going to be proud to tie a black belt around your waist." Tremendous relief swept over him and I asked him to return to class. He left reprimanded but understanding the message. He still felt good about the teacher and good about himself.

Then I brought John back. "I now know what took

place in the back room. I'm very, very proud of Zachary for being honest with me. Honesty is something that all black belts must have, and it was great to see that in one of my students. Once again, tell me what happened."

The young man lowered his head. "Well, sir, I kicked the door."

Again, praise followed as I continued to express how I would always be there for him and that he could always be completely honest with me. "At any point you can turn to me and break the dishonesty cycle."

AMBIGUITY

I remember my younger days in grade school. My teachers repeatedly said, "You have the capability; you're just not performing to your ability. You could do better." This confused me because, obviously, the grades I was receiving were reflective of my ability. In reality, if I had more ability to use my ability, then I would have earned better grades. No one ever seemed to understand it like that. I may have lacked motivation, but no one took the responsibility to change that (and neither did I). They just insisted on aimlessly attacking.

Teachers and coaches need to take responsibility and give children skills. Don't just insist that they're not doing their best; give them specific skills to do better. I avoid saying to students, "That was good, but you're just not trying," or, "What's wrong with you today? Don't you care about what you're doing?"

Whose responsibility is it to motivate the children when they are training on the martial arts floor? The instructors'. If I'm not the one instructing, then it's my responsibility to insure that the instructors on the floor are effectively motivating each student. Challenging students to their outermost limits is essential for them to climb to new heights. We must do it in a supportive, successful manner.

DON'T DO THAT

Don't think of a purple dog.

What are you seeing in your mind right now? A purple dog? If we repeatedly badger our children with what not to do, they only become focused with those negative things. The disks that go around in their drives need to be what *to do*. For example, "sit still," as opposed to, "don't move," "clean your room," as opposed to, "don't let me catch your room messy," "good luck on the test," as opposed to, "don't fail the test."

Spend time listening to what you say to your students. We are often the ones causing the problems by what we say.

CHOICES

I often hear adults telling children to make good choices. Is that a good choice?

Teachers should allow a child to make only *appropriate* choices. Do you want to go to martial arts lessons with your uniform on, or do you want to change once you get there? Do you want to clean your room with your shoes on or with your shoes off? Do you want to practice your moves with the music off or on?

Does it seem empowering to have a six year old make a decision about his future? What did you know at six? Should we expect a six year old to know what is best for him, or should the teachers decide? Often we expect children to know how to act and behave. We should not rely on a child's ability to know how to act in every situation. We should not leave young students to flounder and program their own disks. It's our responsibility to provide guidelines and productive programs from which they can learn.

RESPECT

The most important thing teachers and coaches can do is to respect their students. By respecting students through a nurturing, caring approach, you will understand how to fulfill their every need in the learning process. They say you catch more flies with honey than with vinegar. Being courteous and respectful to children will breed their courtesy and respect toward you. No one likes being badgered. No one likes being repeatedly told what not to do. We need to inform our children of the correct method for learning, for choosing activities, and for interacting with others. Showing young members of our community what it is like to be respected means they will take that information and pass it on to others.

HONESTY

While driving with a fellow martial arts instructor, I noticed a radar detector on his dashboard. As we drove by a police car it sounded an alert. I looked over at him as we engaged in a conversation about teaching children.

"Do you teach your students to be honest?"

"Absolutely," he responded.

"What does the radar detector represent?"

"Oh, that. That's different."

"Is it?"

Children only know what we give them. They become the results of their combined inputs. If an input is dishonest or deceiving, then that type of trait will appear somewhere on their disks.

WHEN TO MAKE UP

If we tell children that it's okay to carry a grudge and get mad, then they will grow up doing just that. Every great person I know has the ability to be stern and not lose control. These great people understand the importance of discipline and are quick to administer it. They are also quick to make up and offer praise. I still remember the only day that my martial arts instructor yelled at me, and I remember as if it were yesterday. I was in the gym at the YMCA standing on a blue mat working with a partner a few years younger. I can repeat for you every word the instructor said, and I can also tell you that from the moment he finished the reprimand he forgot about it.

Every one of my students knows I care about them and that I'm not the type of teacher who gets mad and holds ill feelings for any amount of time. After a correction, reunite with the child and let him know how much you care. Then watch that child grow to do the same.

Chapter Six

Technical Terms

"The biggest failure of all is the person that never tries."
—Dr. Larry Kimsey

In this chapter, we will explore in detail some of my favorite teaching techniques. Each of these technical terms comes with examples of how to apply them in different situations. Log your favorites, and put them to use right away.

PRE-FRAME

Pre-frame describes preparing the child for what is about to happen. For example, on the martial arts floor, "When I say 'go,' you will stand up, answer 'yes, sir,' run to your mark, and stand at attention."

That pre-frame focuses the students' minds by laying down a procedural track. All I have to do then is push a button that plays the disk. When I say, "go," the students stand up, say, "yes, sir," run to their mark, and stand at attention awaiting the next command.

How would a teacher apply this elsewhere? "At

4:00 we're going to piano lessons. I would like you to be inside by 3:30 so that we can get ready. The piano lesson today is going to be very exciting, and remember, this week you are continuing to work on the recital."

Or, "I'm going to ask you all to stand up, place your chair under your desk, quietly walk over to the door, and line up for lunch."

The more pre-frames we give children, the better they understand how to perform and take action. Children want to do what you expect, but sometimes they just forget or lose focus. The pre-frame is a way to remind them of what is expected. Tell a child what you expect of him, and often you'll avoid unwanted behavior.

THE SILENT CORRECTION

Has being told what to do ever annoyed you? It wasn't that you didn't want the information. Rather, it was the voice or the tone used. During pilot training my first instructor pilot had a way of just physically pointing at what I was missing. If we were flying too high, he would point at the altimeter and I corrected the plane. I didn't need him to yell at me. I liked this technique and coined the term, "the silent correction."

You can use this anytime you want a student to make an adjustment. For example, when a student makes a fist and leaves his thumb sticking out, I just point at it. No need to say anything; the student fixes the thumb, and away we go. Once a teacher has laid the correct foundation, a simple point of the finger is an effective reminder. By pointing, the teacher is attacking only one input, visual, leaving the other two, kinesthetic and auditory, alone.

POWER PLAY

Kyle was having trouble at school. He was quiet and not very outgoing. He had been a student at my school for two months when his parents came to me with some concerns. He was having trouble spelling and reading words. He was getting down on himself, and it showed in his other school work.

"He listens to you, Mr. Graybeal." His father said. "Do you have any ideas?"

"Yes, I do." I went on to say that although I couldn't give Kyle direct skills to read and spell in our class that afternoon, I could re-frame him into feeling better about his spelling ability. In addition, I could position his eagerness to learn by stressing the importance of reading.

Throughout the class I asked what books various students liked to read. Luckily I was familiar with most of them, and gave my interpretation of books from *Charlotte's Web* to *Harry the Dirty Dog*. I mentioned how I love to read and how I wish I could have started reading and spelling at their age. I then gave them an assignment to find a book about martial arts and give a report on it.

LEADING

Have you ever seen a student answer a question incorrectly and then clam up, not trying to answer others? When the student does not know the answer, for whatever reason, he can convince himself that trying is not worth it, that he's dumb, and that he can't learn. So, what can a teacher do to insure the students don't clam up? Lead them.

Students should be tested and evaluated. However, in the learning stages teachers may want to convey to students that they are there to teach and support the learning process. For example, "How many separate moves are there in a front kick?" the teacher asks the class.

Jimmy raises his hand, and total confusion blankets his face. He forgot the answer. The teacher has a few options. One, call on someone else. Two, tell the student the answer. Three, lead the student through a remembering process. When Jimmy's face sagged in embarrassment, the teacher slipped four fingers to his side. In essence, he was leading the student to the right answer through a process that helped him remember in the future.

Jimmy smiles and yells out, "Four."

Do you think Jimmy will listen and be excited to give his next answer?

There are appropriate times that teachers can lead students, just as there are inappropriate times.

FUTURE BUILDING

"Future building" is a term I use to thrust a student into an event that has not yet happened. By doing this the student can see, feel, and hear the events that take place at the completion of a goal. I build the "Black Belt" goal into each and every class. This goal may not be achieved for several years. Nevertheless, I lead the student through steps to get the feeling now and build what I call a compelling future, a future that becomes vivid and realistic. Give your students a clear picture of the future, and watch it become a reality.

If you were a medical doctor, you would have a

pretty good idea of what it took to get there. As a coach you can lead someone into the future so he gets an idea of what it takes to get where he wants to go. I asked one of my older students these questions one afternoon.

"So, you want to be a doctor?"

"Yes, I've been thinking about it," the student answered.

"Let's say you were a doctor. What do you think you would have done to get to where you are?"

"I guess I would have taken the first step like calling some medical schools and finding out what it takes to get accepted."

This conversation continued off and on for several hours. A coach or teacher can take a student forward in time to experience events that have not yet taken place simply by asking a few questions. Put yourself in a position five years in the past, knowing what you know now. Would you be anywhere different?

I always like to ask children what they are going to be when they grow up. I don't stop with one answer. For your future to be compelling, it must be vivid and real.

"Jimmy, what do you want to be when you grow up?" the teacher asks.

Jimmy bites his lip and answers, "A fireman."

The teacher can put Jimmy into his future now by asking a few more questions. "What kind of fireman would you be? What kind of fire truck would you drive? Would it be red or that new yellow color?"

MATCHING AND MIRRORING

When communicating with children, don't forget

to match and mirror them. People are in rapport when they act alike. When a teacher wants to establish a deep level of one-on-one communication, match the student's head position, body position, and mannerisms. Watch how the student moves and then move alike. This is not mimicking. It's a way to enter the same mental state as the child and allow him to feel closer to the teacher.

A young man challenged me one afternoon. He was about as energetic as they come. One by one I went through each of my techniques trying to establish a bond with this fiery four year old. Each time I switched gears, he stayed one step ahead of me. I was getting nowhere. He stopped running and dropped down to the ground, playing with a small truck he had brought with him.

I decided to start matching and mirroring him. I sat down on the floor exactly like him. I started breathing like him, and I put on the same facial expression. I attempted to enter a like state.

Within a few seconds, the young man looked up at me and cocked his head to the left. That was all it took. We spent the next few minutes talking about his truck and then I showed him around the school. By the time I finished the tour, he was ready for the lesson to begin.

Matching and mirroring is a wonderful way to establish rapport. Gain confidence in your students' minds that you understand them and relate to them.

THE CHALLENGE

Everyone loves a challenge. When working with young students, the teacher can use a challenge to get the students to "prove him wrong." It's similar to hearing an adult say, "I'll bet you can't do this." When presenting a student with a new task or skill, align it with a challenge that will enhance and quicken the learning process.

Presenting a challenge in the proper way is important. It's important to have a look on your face that lets the student know that the challenge is somewhat light-hearted. You don't want the child to think that you really believe they can't do it.

For example: "That kick was really good. Could you kick twice without putting your foot down?"

THE SURPRISE

When I have a student do something I think is important and I want him to remember, I will act completely astonished and surprised. Often teachers take the joy of learning for granted. Children become excited about learning new things, and they want to know they are special. It's this joy that we want to extend. So the next time a student uses his new knowledge, show him, tell him, and allow him to feel your excitement.

DISTRACTION

A young child's mind has a sense of urgency. What's happening at that moment is, of course, the most important. Have you ever seen a child bump her toe and become completely unable to continue a normal pattern of activity? If a student succumbs to a small event that takes on monstrous momentum, distract and refocus her mind.

Tommy came to me because his eye hurt. I asked what happened, and he told me that his karate belt had flipped up and hit him in the eye. I checked the eye calmly to insure there was no damage and then began my distraction process.

"Okay, your eye hurts now. Yet what would happen if I stepped on your foot. Do you think that your foot would hurt more than your eye?" I'll often step lightly on the student's foot to cause a change in feeling, breaking his pattern. Or, "Okay, your eye hurts, but what do you think would happen if you stepped on my toe. Do you think my foot would hurt more than your eye? Go ahead and step on my foot."

By no means should you ignore the student's problem, because *you* are responsible for the well-being of your students. But in a minor incident these suggestions generally get students to laugh and move forward.

STATE CHANGE

During a recent student promotional testing at the martial arts school, a youngster in the back raised his hand. "Excuse me, sir," in a very nervous voice, "Will we still get our new belts if we don't pass our test?" Panic engulfed his face.

I walked over to him, grabbed his shoulders, spun him around gently, and then whispered to him while I continued to touch him in a supportive manner. "There's no need to worry about that. You're one of my best students. The skill level you display in class is far superior to what is needed today at this evaluation."

The look on the child's face changed instantly; I

had altered his state.

When a child enters an unproductive state, we immediately need to change it. I use several techniques to do that, the most important of which is the physiological shift. Ask the child to stand up and turn around. Ask the child to do ten jumping jacks. Ask the child to shake her head or leg, or walk up to a child and gently and playfully jostle him or spin him around. All these actions will cause a shift in his physiology and, therefore, a state change. In essence, the teacher is bumping the drive and changing the disk he is playing.

One of the most enjoyable ways to change a state is through the use of laughter. During a New Year's Eve lock-in at my martial arts school, an instructor sent two young boys, Billy and Timmy, over to me. While sitting on a stool observing the children, I asked them if they were having a good time.

Billy, the older boy who had just joined the martial arts school, responded, "I was just sitting there, and suddenly my hand flew off and hit him in the head. I was just minding my own business. I don't know what happened." He began to cry.

The other little boy, Timmy, started to cry also and said, "Well, he was kicking at me, and then I just kind of kicked back at him."

The two boys were cousins, and their parents had both approached me prior to the lock-in expressing concern that they had been together all weekend, and they might get on each other's nerves.

As the boys were telling the story there was no winning. I determined no one was truly at fault, and it was just a case of "boys being boys." I decided to change their state, which I did by laughing. I'm sure you can imagine how funny this story was. This little boy's hand flew off on its own and hit his friend in the head. I started to laugh, not a little laugh, but a huge belly laugh. I was laughing so hard that I fell off my stool. The two little boys began laughing with me and laughed so hard they fell to the floor also. They were laughing so hard they couldn't even look at me. After about two minutes of laughing, I pulled myself back up on the stool and watched them go join the rest of the students. They didn't have any other problems the rest of the night.

Simply finding something that will change the student's state will often change the student's ability to learn. The state change can take on many different aspects and revolves around the teacher's ability to scratch the disk.

THE INTENSE MOMENT

Like all aspects of praise, sharing an intense moment with your students creates a greater bond. An intense moment is where the student and the teacher come together, and the teacher focuses on the visual, auditory, and kinesthetic inputs of the student. Speed, noise, and intense eye contact are aspects of a brief moment where the teacher and the student tune out all other inputs. I like to grab the student and look deeply into his eyes as I tell him he has what it takes to be a great black belt. This blocks out all other stimuli. You want to convey to the student that he is the only one in the world at that moment.

THE BELLOW

When I see a child looking out the window, off in

dream land, I take responsibility. Something isn't keeping the child's attention. So how do I regain his focus? Bellowing the student's name works wonderfully. When the child refocuses, I smile and quietly ask her how she's doing.

My father was a master of the bellow, especially out the back door. I would get on the school bus in the morning, and neighbors who lived over a half mile away would ask me what I had gotten in trouble for the previous night. The bellow allows us to correct a child by attacking the behaviors, not the child.

A bellow is a way to correct the child sometimes without even specifically addressing him. In our school when two students face each other, we insist no one walk between them since an injury could result if they suddenly began to spar. So when I see a student walk between two others, I bellow a loud noise which causes everyone to check what they are doing. The student who walked between the others will confirm that he made a mistake and recover.

But, let me add a caveat to the bellow. Never yell at a child. The bellow is a state change technique, not a conversation, reprimand, or teaching voice. It's just a noise intended to provoke a state change, to skip the disk being played.

Why not just yell? A father brought an interesting technique to my attention. He had a three year old son, and when he leaned over and whispered to his son, the boy acted instantly. The father explained that long ago he had made a pact with himself, a goal, that he would never yell at his son. By speaking in a normal tone of voice, or even a whisper, he got a much better response.

THE SILENT BELLOW

As I discussed earlier, facial expressions are important tools for communicating with children. The silent bellow is a facial expression made without verbal noise. A simple look at a child can skip or scratch the disk she's playing. Identify the expression and link it to a verbal correction, and you will have a powerful, silent way to adjust the disk she is playing.

CONDITIONED RESPONSE—ANCHOR

An anchor is a method used to elicit a certain response. Think back to a song you enjoy which makes you think of a specific time or an event, or a time when you shook hands with someone and instantly remembered someone else. That is an anchor.

Erin slipped and fell one day as she ran across the floor in an afternoon martial arts class. She burst into tears as her head lightly bounced off the padded floor. She entered a kinesthetic state (looking down) and started to cry. I took her aside, checked her head carefully to insure there was no physical injury, then jostled her gently to skip the disk she was playing (state change), and had her look up. Looking up forced her into a visual state away from the kinesthetic state she was in while crying.

She recovered and went back to class. When her mother came in after class, I walked Erin over and made the mistake of telling her mother what happened. This took Erin back in time to when she had fallen on the floor. I had effectively thrown that old disk back into her drive which returned her to her previous kinesthetic state. Erin began crying. Her mother knelt down and accepted Erin into her arms. This caused the child's head to drop. The kinesthetic state was reinforced, and the crying increased.

Often teachers reinforce events that are not empowering. Instead, we must look at each situation differently and work with the student, making sure we structure events with positive outcomes.

To develop positive anchors, I always praise children in three areas—auditory, visual, and kinesthetic. I'll make sure that I say something to them, produce a special facial expression, a thumbs-up or a proud look, and a touch. I often touch them on their shoulder and eventually create a conditioned response—an anchor. Our goal is to anchor those good feelings the child has when being praised and bring them back with a simple touch. Eventually that touch will create good feelings without saying a word.

SPINNING

Spinning a student's mind is an effective way to bring a student back into focus. To spin a student's mind is to cause a brief moment of confusion by questioning his actions when he is distracted from the task at hand. The confusion quickly brings about a re-focusing.

For example, Jake was looking out the window in class one day. I asked what he was doing. He stared back at me in total confusion, his mind spinning.

"Why were you looking out the window?" I asked again.

Jake stared back, still searching for an answer.

"Jake, answer my question. Why were you looking out the window?"

"Uh, I don't know, sir."

"I know you don't know, but what if you did know? I mean, there has to be a reason. There is a reason for everything."

This line of questioning is done not to badger the student. It allows the student to search his own mind for a reason for looking out the window. I don't expect the student to answer. The technique gives him an opportunity to correct himself and think about was he was doing. To understand is basic. By asking leading questions, we can spin the child's mind back into focus.

REDIRECT

A dad came to me once with his little girl following close behind. The dad began, "Go ahead, tell him."

I looked at the child, "What's going on?"

She looked down and responded, "Nothing."

Her dad pushed her forward from behind his leg and said, "No. You're here now; go ahead and tell him."

"Well, I want to quit."

I smiled and asked her to come into the office. I had her sit down, and then I took the seat next to hers, close to eye-level, and asked, "What was this again? Can you tell me one more time?"

"Well, I want to quit," she answered hesitantly in a quiet voice.

I put a tremendous smile on my face. "That's great. That's the most exciting thing I quite possibly have ever heard." She brought her eyes up with a confused look on her face. "Hey, you know what? You cannot become a black belt until you want to quit. You're a green belt. I didn't want to quit until I was a brown belt."

I opened the door and had her walk out to the floor. I then had her look up at the wall where we have all of our colored belts, white through black, hanging in order. "Look where you are. Look where brown belt is. You're three belts ahead of me. That's absolutely incredible. I'm very proud of you."

Still a little confused, I took her back to the office and sat her down. "Look, becoming a black belt is something very special. You must endure struggles along the way. That's what it means to be a black belt—to overcome struggle. You must learn to overcome adversities, and wanting to quit is one of the major adversities. Young lady, now you are set. Your destiny has been put in place. You will be a black belt."

She walked out of the office, and her dad asked, "Well, are you still quitting?"

She looked up with a wide grin on her face and said, "No, sir; I'm going to be a black belt."

At the writing of this book, nine months have passed and she is doing wonderfully in the school.

Forcing

Last week, a wonderful student wanted to quit. After some investigation and speaking with the parents and the student, I discovered why. He felt that if he wanted to stay in martial arts and be successful, he had to change his behavior at home from one of misbehaving to one of behaving. He didn't want to do that, so he asked to quit. Unfortunately, his parents had decided that quitting was okay. I had failed to convey the importance of the Support Triangle effectively to them. I truly believe that no child ever quits. Rather, the support structure around them fails. His mother came into the school, and we sat down for a talk. I asked the mother, "Do you remember our discussion about applying leverage to your son?"

"Yes, it was very helpful at first, but the more we brought up your name the more he didn't want to come to class."

"Let's assume he doesn't want to change, and he doesn't want to lose face in front of his instructors. So he wants to quit."

"Yes, I can see that."

"I would like to set up a time to visit with him. When would be a good time for you?"

"No, that would be too difficult for him." She answered. "He wanted me to tell you that he's quitting."

"Of course it's difficult. However, it's a decision he made, and he should come in and confront that decision."

"Oh, that would be too hard for him."

I leaned over and lowered my voice. "In eight years when your son is fifteen and has a difficult struggle in life, do you want him to have experience dealing with difficult situations?"

"Well, I'm not going to force him to talk to you. It would be too tough on him."

"What do you think we do in class every day? We force the students to do everything from lift their leg a little higher to stand there and not move for thirty seconds."

"I know. This is a wonderful program."

"Then why are you letting a seven year old child choose what's best for him? Would you allow him to choose not to go to school?"

"Of course not."

"Why would you let him choose not to come to martial arts if it's beneficial?"

She then repeated, "Well, I can't force him."

"Forcing, motivating, coaching, leading, whatever you want to call it, it's all the same. It just so happens that when adults don't want to go through with the commitments they've made, they say it's 'forcing.' When they do want to go through with it, they call it 'motivating.'"

With truly supportive programs and truly supportive parents, the idea of quitting never comes up. When we tell a child that quitting is okay, we instill quitting qualities.

Daniel, a five year old boy, was about a month into the program at my school. He didn't want to go to martial arts class one evening, but his mother brought him to class anyway. His mother carried him out to the middle of the workout floor, put him down at attention position, and walked over to one side. Daniel started crying. Class lasted forty-five minutes and he cried most of the time.

The instructors worked with him, trying to motivate him and change his pattern. We would change it only for a few minutes, and then he would start crying again. His mother stayed to the side. It was a tough situation to see a little boy cry like that, but it was perhaps the most beneficial thing his mother ever did for him.

First of all, she reinforced the fact that he was not in control. The mother was in control, and he, the son, was going to do what the mother said. Understanding discipline is important. Discipline means learning, and the mother was enlightening the son with discipline for him to learn. Two months later, Daniel was the student of the month. He is a wonderfully focused child and has turned out to be a great martial artist.

I was recently visiting with a friend of mine, and we were discussing the ins and outs of coaching children. I told her that my children will take martial arts lessons.

She responded, "What if they don't want to? You can't force them."

I looked back at her. "Oh, yes I can. I'm the parent, and my children will."

"If you force them, they'll resent you."

She danced competitively for fourteen years until college and was adamant that her parents never forced her to continue.

"How do you know your parents never forced you to continue to dance?" I asked. "When we don't want to do something, we often say it is forcing. When you truly want them to do something it just happens, like going to school. Have you ever heard a child say he or she didn't want to go to school?"

"Yes, of course."

"Do you believe the parents think of it as forcing their children to go to school?"

"I saw kids who were forced to dance. They hated it and their parents. My parents never forced me."

"How do you know they weren't forcing you? Maybe they were so good at forcing that you never even knew it. If a parent believes in a program, there generally is no problem getting the child to continue."

The reason I ask those types of questions is simple. If we build barriers and block different angles in our thinking, then we'll get the same results as others. If we look to the situation differently without blinders and ask non-limiting questions, then we may see a new approach, one which is empowering.

SILENCE

Perhaps the most overlooked aspect of teaching is the use of non-verbal communication. As I teach class each night, my face goes through a full range of expressions. I'll show the new students each of the facial expressions I use on their first day in class. "This is my proud face. This is my happy face. This is my excited face. This is my confused face." Once children know how to bring a facial expression to the teacher, they try hard to earn a proud face.

THE GLOSS OVER

If an adult makes a big deal out of something, we effectively lay down a pattern of importance. For example, I'll often get children in the martial arts school who are reluctant to do much of anything, especially walking onto the martial arts floor and joining class.

"I don't want to do it," the new student says to her mother.

If the parent reinforces the new student's panic by asking a question like, "You don't want to do it? Why not? Oh, go on, it'll be fun. I know the kids are bigger than you but..." The parents unknowingly legitimize the child's reluctance.

When a child says he doesn't want to join the class, I gloss over it. I pretend the child said nothing and continue. I kneel down and look him in the eyes. "Just put your shoes and socks over there." I'll touch him on the shoulder to get a physical shift and get him moving toward the training floor.

I asked a young girl to warm up the class one

afternoon and received no response from her. She froze. Standing in front of everyone and speaking caused her great concern.

"I don't want to do it."

"That's okay, just go up in the front and tell them to start doing front kicks."

In a respectful way, I challenged her to perform at the outer limits of her comfort range. I glossed over what she said and acted like it was nothing. If I had questioned her and dwelled on that issue, it would have done nothing but reinforce her panic.

Jason was three when he started lessons, and it took him a few classes to really get going. When he came out to the floor I could tell he was still apprehensive to begin. His mother and father watched from the side as Jason stood ready for class.

I lined the class up in front of a large kicking pad. One by one the students came forward and kicked. After Jason kicked, he turned to me and told me that he wanted to sit by his mother. I answered, "Okay, go back to the end of the line." Jason looked at me and ran back to the end of the line. He did this well over ten times, and I glossed over what he said each time. If I had made a big deal out of it by asking, "Why?" I would have reinforced his desire to be with his mom.

By no means am I saying that we should not be compassionate with our students. What I am saying is that we need to provide a structured, supportive environment that will enable our students to learn and experience new feelings, thereby empowering them.

INTERRUPTIONS

When I'm involved in a conversation and a child

interrupts, I take one second and look down at the child, creating a one-on-one intense moment. I ask him to remember what he wants to tell me. Then I remind the student I'm currently holding a conversation with someone else, but if he would wait I would love to hear what he has to say. I return to finish the conversation. Afterwards, I lower myself to his eye level and ask him what he wishes to say. If the student says, "Oh, I forgot," I'll grab him to jiggle his disk drive and say, "Well, let's pretend you didn't forget. What did you want to say?"

This type of approach reinforces the bond between the teacher and the child. It teaches the child respect and communicates I care about him in a supportive manner.

PATENT PRAISES

As we discussed earlier, teachers should attack all three inputs when they praise a child. Praise is more than just telling a child she's doing a wonderful job. We have all seen the charts that list one hundred ways to praise a child, but they are only words. For true praise, you need much more.

Some of my favorites are:

The Victory Lap

The child runs around the class as everyone claps. Running stimulates the kinesthetic input. Clapping together with a verbal command to "Take a victory lap" stimulates the auditory input, and the sight of hands coming together stimulates the visual input.

The Victory Flip

Standing behind the child, the teacher picks him up in the air and twirls him around. This is, of course, done with smaller children.

The Pat on the Back

When I pat a child on the back, it's different from an everyday light touch. It's powerful and intense.

The Self-Pat on the Back

Congratulating the students isn't only important for the teacher; it's just as important for the students to congratulate themselves. I have the students stand at attention while I tell them, "Raise your right hand high in the air and lower it behind your back. Now pat yourself on the back."

Personal Trivia

Intense, one-on-one moments with a child will stick in his or her mind. Questions like, "What did you have to eat today?" or, "What is your dog's name?" will communicate to the child you care about him. I often ask what the child ate and tell him to eat it again the next day because he is doing such a good job. All are ways to have intense moments together.

Find out as much as you can about your students—the names of their dogs, their middle names, and what they like to do. The more you know about a student, the more the student knows you care. The more you know about a student, the better you'll understand what makes him who he is.

I have a young student named Greg. He's only six years old, but on the weekends he rock climbs with his parents. Often I will ask how the rock climbing is going, but I don't stop there. I enter a conversation with him about the specifics of rock climbing. I ask what the equipment is called and what commands are used. By asking questions that require exact and specific answers I am able to create a vivid and compelling future.

INDEPENDENT REMINDERS

We must not badger children. We must be supportive and offer guidance. Helping a child remember to correct certain traits or enhance others takes a special approach. The best way is to have the child remember by herself so the teacher does not become harassing.

Teaching a child to stop biting her fingernails might work by first encouraging the child to have a discussion about what her goals are. Once the child agrees that she wants to stop, coach her with techniques to remember the goal. Put a band around her wrist, and each time she brings her hand to her mouth she'll see the band and remember the goal. Or have the third party (i.e. martial arts teacher) bring the nail-biting to the child's attention. Parents can play off the leverage I assert over the students and encourage the child by using the third party. Pointing to the child's fingers each time she brings her hand to her mouth will remind her with just one input. The fewer inputs a teacher uses to remind a child, the more likely the child will accept the correction and feel good about the teacher.

LINKING

I use several different methods to help children remember new knowledge. I have them wear a watch or take something special to school and place it on their desk. Every time they see the object, they'll independently remember what they should be doing. We can remember our new techniques the same way. Hang something special from your rear view mirror so that every time you get into your car you consciously think about remembering to use these new techniques.

The name of one of our martial arts styles is Tae Kwon Do. It is a Korean word meaning foot, hand, art. We get children to remember foot-hand-art by linking the sign language sign for foot, hand, and art together with the words. By linking a kinesthetic pattern and a visual movement to words, the three inputs join together, increasing the ability to recall.

There are endless possibilities for this type of linking. Remember that most children don't know sign language, so the link does not have to make sense. In our Tiny Tigers class for three and four year olds, we use this principle with the student oath. The children learn "knowledge in the mind, honesty in the heart, and strength in the body," by putting their hands on their heads when they say "knowledge in the mind," hands on their hearts when they say "honesty in the heart," and hands at their sides when they say "strength in the body."

COMPELLING FUTURE

We use the "black belt" as an anchor for the future.

The words "black belt" create in the child's mind a vision of excellence. By finding something a child is doing right and praising him, you can link his actions to a desire to please. Far too often we wait to talk to a child until he's doing something wrong. When the child does something wrong, we give him what he needs—quality time or the one-on-one intense moments together.

Instead of dwelling on what happens when a student does something wrong, focus on what he does right. Constantly reinforce the values that you want him to have for the rest of his life. Make those grooves on the disks in his mind deeper and deeper. When someone tries to reformat that disk and record destructive tracks, the child will be so strong that his values won't be compromised.

Chapter Seven

Secret Techniques

"You could not step twice into the same rivers; for other waters are ever flowing on to you."
—Heraclitus

QUESTIONING

When I teach a class, I often start by asking a question, nothing major, just something to engage each student's mind and get them searching for answers. The quest for information helps keep the student motivated and focused. Yesterday I started a sparring class by asking the best way for me to close the distance into striking distance of my opponent. "Have you ever wondered how planes fly?" would be a great way to introduce the theory of flight. "Do you know how plants grow?" would be a wonderful way to introduce a child to gardening.

ROLE PLAYING

Role playing allows children to prepare for many

situations they're likely to encounter. You wouldn't want to fly an F-16 without having practiced what to do if you encounter a Russian MiG-29. That's a combat scenario a fighter pilot practices often. Our children encounter combat scenarios every day when they're faced with decisions about drugs, sex, and cheating, to name a few.

Set up practices where a student can feel, say, and see exactly what a situation might be like. Set up a role playing exercise that has a bully. The bully tries his or her best to do what bullies do, and your student practices ways to deal with him. Use these role playing exercises daily and remember to make them vivid, loud, and real.

Instead of having students sit and listen to someone inform them about drugs, have them role play an encounter with so-called friends offering them drugs. Let the students learn how to interact and effectively decline. And remember that the more senses a teacher can put into a lesson, the more the students will take away from that lesson.

Kurt is a brown-haired three year old. The other day he went to the back room and filled a cup of water from the water cooler. He then took that cup of water out to the workout area of our martial arts school. We don't allow students to drink water on the floor. I was about to say something when his mother called his name. Kurt either didn't hear or simply didn't listen, because he didn't stop. I called to him as well but also received no response. I walked onto the floor and physically guided Kurt back to the water cooler. "Did you hear us calling you?"

"Yes."

I took away the cup, which caused a loud noise from somewhere inside this small person. I had interrupted his pattern and once he calmed, I began a series of questions.

"Did you know that you were not supposed to drink water on the workout floor?"

"No." He looked away.

"If you are drinking water and happen to spill it, someone might slip and fall and get hurt.

When your mother or I call you, you should come immediately. Okay?"

"Yes, sir."

"Let's try this again." I gave him a cup of water and sent him toward the workout floor.

"Kurt," I called.

Young Kurt turned and walked back toward me. I praised him for listening so well. He got a chance to practice his new information and be rewarded. These steps are more time consuming than just yelling, but you'll be ahead of the game when the student knows exactly what the teacher expects. Instead of shouting without gaining the desired results, you'll have a child who is empowered with new knowledge.

NICKNAMES

In the Air Force, everyone had a call sign—a name that identified the pilot. Sometimes the call signs were linked to a specific event in the pilots' lives. I knew one pilot who had a tendency to fly planes in which, for no apparent reason, the bomb racks would fall off. We called him Rack. Some pilots' call signs related to their body stature. "Plank" was the call sign for one very tall pilot. Others used a derivative of their real names. McDonnell quickly became Mac.

Giving students nicknames creates a special bond

between the teacher and the child, and learning increases. Some students long for nicknames, and parents will secretly tell me of their son's or daughter's desire to have one. The names must come from the moment and must fit in order to stick. This technique is a fun way to tell that child he or she is special.

THE INPUTS

A few years ago, I had the opportunity to walk on fire. Before we took our first step over the hot coals the coach told me and the 1,500 others to say, "cool maas," over and over. When someone asked why, the coach said, "cool maas is better than hot maas." We all agreed. By saying the same thing over and over, our minds pushed out other thoughts including the fact we were standing on red-hot coals!

If we say something over and over, we can cancel out other inputs and concentrate on one single thought. When I'm teaching, I'll have the students repeat a particular word during each move. This helps their minds to focus on the task at hand, avoiding thoughts about food, the snow outside, or their upcoming field trip. Therefore we have a much more productive and focused class.

Use this to your advantage. In gymnastics have the children repeat their names or repeat the word, "balance," over and over. When children are playing basketball have them say, "dribble," every time they dribble the ball. In our classes we have them say, "boom," or, "pow," during set patterns or moves each time they kick or punch.

MOTION CREATING EMOTION

Most kinesthetic states we enter are of a ho-hum nature and not very lively. When students move around, they change from a low energy kinesthetic state into an energized visual state. When I visit one of my student's grade schools, I instruct the entire class to stand up and start moving.

I prefer to teach a class that gives me feedback, and I receive the most feedback from a class of students whose blood is pumping and minds are charged. Each child energizes the others, and it eventually comes back to me as the teacher.

Keep your classes moving. An energized class will learn more.

STORY TIME

I had a student named Ryan who just didn't want to participate in the class one day. I used this story to get him going.

There were three baby eagles in a nest with Papa Eagle and Mama Eagle. One morning Mama Eagle came to the three little eagles and told them it was their turn to fly. The first eagle, Iron Claw, ran to the edge of the nest and jumped off, soaring as if he had been flying for years. The next baby eagle was Flying Feather. He jumped off the nest and soared without a problem, landing smoothly back on the nest. Little Beak was last. Mama Eagle called for him to come to the edge of the nest, but Little Beak did not move. "I'm far too small to fly," he said, frozen in his place in the nest. "I don't think I can do it."

To that Mama Eagle responded, "Oh, you'll be all

right. Your two brothers flew just fine. Give it a try."

"No way." Little Beak hid his head.

With that, Papa Eagle stepped forward and with his deep voice called to Little Beak. "You are an eagle, and all eagles fly. Your grandfather was a small eagle like you, and he was one of the best flyers around. Now step up to the edge of the nest."

Little Beak did what his father told him. He moved to the edge of the nest and closed his eyes.

"Now flap your wings," Father Eagle called.

Little Beak flapped and flapped. Then he cried out, "Father, I can't feel the nest."

"Open your eyes, Little Beak. You are flying."

And did Little Beak fly! He flew high and low, upside down and right side up. The other eagles in the nest were speechless. They had just seen the unbelievable.

I then began to ask Ryan questions. "Why didn't Little Beak want to fly? Who helped him to gain the courage to fly? Is there anything you've ever done that at first you didn't want to try? Who are some of the people who can help you when you need encouragement?"

This story is simple. Ryan got the message loud and clear. He went to work and had a class he'll never forget.

THE LAST IMPRESSION MUST BE POSITIVE

A good teacher wants students not only to remember what they are taught, but to also think positively of the teacher. How do you do that? I received a call one afternoon from Mr. Peterson, a local grade school principal. He asked me if I could meet with him about Jeff, an eight year old who had been my student for about two months. I arrived at the school to discover that he had been fighting, a violation of a strict rule at our martial arts school.

After the principal and parents finished with him it was my turn. I asked the principal if there was a room we could use, and he pointed to a small room off to the side. I entered the pink brick room noting that there was nothing on the walls. There were only two chrome chairs facing each other which, at the time, was appropriate indeed. I sat facing the door, and Jeff faced me. It was so quiet I could hear the clock across the hall ticking through the closed door.

I let the tension build and then asked the first question, "What happened?"

Jeff took a deep breath and started his story. He told of an older boy who had pushed him in the hallway. I asked him to describe the incident, including the surroundings, in more detail, and we both determined the fight was avoidable.

I gave him a verbal reprimand then went into how he could have avoided the situation and, most importantly, how to avoid similar situations in the future. The last thing I said to Jeff was that he was doing well in martial arts. I wanted him to leave with a positive feeling about his experience with me and the fact that he had learned new skills for dealing with difficult encounters.

VOICE INFLECTION

Remember that tonality, or voice inflection, is the second most important part of external communication. By placing different emphases on words, you can make your point. It is difficult to focus your attention on or toward someone who sounds like a computer.

A BIG DEAL

I watched Tracy, a seven year old, help a younger student put on her safety equipment. It was a wonderful sight to see the two sitting on the floor working to get the elastic straps around their feet. I stopped class and told everyone to stand at attention. I called Tracy up to the front of the class and proceeded to shower her with praise. I made a big deal out of her helping the other student. I made it such a big deal that when I finished my lavish praise, the other students raced to find someone to help.

Whenever I see a student do something that I want him to do again, I make a big deal out of it. Take the time to catch the child doing something good, and etch that trait deeply on his disk. In many children's lives the mistakes become the big deal. Resolve to find something positive in your students each and every day, and you will empower their lives.

Chapter Eight

Are We Judging a Book by Its Cover?

"A new word is like a fresh seed sown on the ground of the discussion."
—Ludwig Wittgenstein

Judging a child by what someone else says is too easy and happens too often. If someone introduces a student as being ADD, do you expect something different from him? Do you give less? What someone tells you about a child can be distinctly different from who that child really is. It is our responsibility as teachers to learn about each child and not hold them back or give them less attention based on a preconceived notion or idea.

I have over two hundred children in my martial arts school. Of those, about sixty-five have been tagged by someone as having some form of ADD or ADHD. Of those sixty-five, as many as thirty are on some type of medication. Is that too many? I have seen children walk through our door completely lethargic, and I often wonder who is taking responsibility for rearing those children. Is it the doctor, the

117

teacher, the parent, or the drugs?

"Words are, of course, the most powerful drug used by mankind."
—Rudya rd Kipling

LABELS

I often see ADD/ADHD used as an excuse for someone's failure to orchestrate the proper learning environment. Every child is different. Therefore, we must teach every child differently. I believe that every child can focus, listen, and learn regardless of a label. It is very important for someone in each child's life to truly believe that the child can do things on his own. If a student is not focusing in class, I must take some kind of action. I change my approach or examine my communication process. I must take full responsibility for the fact that the child is not focusing and find a solution.

Does that mean that certain children do not have difficulty focusing? No. Saying that medication associated with these labels does not improve the lives of certain children would simply not be true. And by no means is this a message that a child should discontinue the use of his medication without first seeing his doctor.

I have read a tremendous amount of literature on ADD/ADHD and have heard numerous theories, including speculation that the condition is the result of a chemical imbalance or even that it is a myth. While many are working to find the answer, I'm not going to wait. Regardless of what it is or what causes it, I still must create a supportive and structured environment geared toward empowering children.

I encourage you to look for motivating and enhancing techniques to empower children. I take full responsibility for motivating, leading, disciplining, and creating the conditions in which children can develop the successful qualities which make them productive members of society. I try not to let labels—even ADD or ADHD—get in the way.

I was discussing this topic with a new parent in my school the other day. She told me that the teachers at her son's school insist that he has attention problems. When she suggested that the child might just be bored, the teachers took offense. If a child is bored in my class, I take responsibility for it. I don't blame the child. If you want to be a great teacher, start by looking inside before you reach for an excuse and label a child because you have not been able to reach him.

MAGIC

We must be aware of the advice we receive about how best to work with our students. All teachers must first analyze and understand the techniques or advice they get.

I have heard of a technique in which teachers give children a count of three by which time they are expected to modify the inappropriate behavior they had been demonstrating. In my opinion, the count should start and end with three.

Yes, it is important to remind children the proper way to behave, and yes, we should explain any new rules or guidelines we are going to use. But if you tell a child they don't have to obey until three, what do you think they're going to do?

By all means, remind your students of proper

behavior. Help them learn in a truly supportive and productive environment. But don't become lenient. Stay focused and regimented.

Don't spend your day counting.

If there is a need for punishment, administer it.

If there is a need for guidance, guide.

If there is a need for praise, praise.

Chapter Nine

Sudden Victory

"What lies behind us and what lies before us are tiny matters compared to what lies within us."
—Ralph Waldo Emerson

YOU GO FIRST. NO, YOU GO FIRST

At a staff meeting one afternoon my fellow instructors and I discussed the student of the month. We determined that it should be Katie. She had been with us for about two years and had experienced the full extent of the martial arts. Everyone in her life was supportive of her involvement, which was creating a terrific cycle. There was one day when her behavior particularly caught our attention.

Whether her outstanding performance was because of our praise or whether we praised her for her performance and moved her forward is the question. Which came first? All that matters is that we praised her performance, she performed at higher and higher levels, and we continued our praise. She became exceptional. That's the goal.

121

I looked at her in the middle of class and said, "You have super focus today. Don't change a thing." I showered her with praise for what she was doing. At the end of class I brought her up to the front, took off my black belt, and tied it around her waist. I took a picture of us and put it up on our bulletin board.

Today she is even more focused and more driven. There is no stopping her. She can run an entire forty-five minute class from start to finish by herself. She can put drills and exercises together for a great workout. As she bounces across the floor I have to remember that Katie is only six years old.

Sitting around the conference table we asked ourselves, "Who is responsible for making this young girl a superstar?" Is it the instructors who decided all of a sudden to take her aside and praise her lavishly? Or is it Katie herself who on her own made a commitment that she was going to look sharp and be wonderful? I don't have an answer to that question, but it is sure a fun experiment. Find a child, smother her with praise, sit back, and watch what happens.

"Success seems to be largely a matter of hanging on after others have let go."
—William Feather

IT'S OUR JOB

If we lose sight of the leaders, then our team will not be prepared for battle.

As a child walks down the road of life, our job is to bump that child back onto the road when he or she strays. As time goes on the deviations become less and less, and the child becomes even more focused towards the destination—success. We can't be every child's parent. What we hope to become is every child's mentor.

That little explanation makes it sound so easy, although we know in reality that nothing works overnight. It only works when someone takes action, has the ability to change, knows how to communicate effectively, takes full, one hundred percent responsibility, and has a thirst for new knowledge.

Find a program that is enhancing for children. Coach them to stay with that program. I see the most value in programs that can give children skills for life. What if the child wants to stop doing what the teacher feels is valuable? Once again, I truly believe that no child ever quits. The support structure around that child fails. Don't fail your students.

When I was eight years old, my parents purchased a piano and asked me if I wanted to take lessons. I took piano lessons for one month, and then I wanted to quit. To this day I cannot play the piano well. I have always regretted my parents' decision to let me quit. I think back on it now and wish they had effectively motivated me, coached me, led me, or forced me, whatever word you want to use, to become a piano player. Is there a similar skill you wanted to learn but quit? Have you let students in your life quit? Are those qualities you want them to have? If you accept quitting in your life, then you must expect it from your students.

Remember each person's job. The parents are the parents. The teachers are the teachers. The students are the students. It is the child's job to want to quit. That's what they are supposed to do. It's their job to want to do one thing one day and something else the next.

As adults what we must do is guide, coach, enhance, and motivate. Stick by your decisions about what is best **for** them, so we can instill the best **in** them. Who knows more about what is better for a child? Is it the child who has only spent a limited number of years on the earth or the adult who has infinitely more knowledge and experiences to pass on?

"You cannot escape the responsibility of tomorrow by evading it today."
—Abraham Lincoln

There is no question in my mind that a great many things had to happen to put this information together. I had not been to church for most of the winter. I spent Sundays pheasant hunting with my dog. My first day in church after hunting season I heard a particularly good sermon about "Protecting Our Children." Of all the sermons that I could have possibly heard, I heard one about protecting children and enhancing their lives.

Once you realize your goals and understand your purpose on the earth, it is interesting how fate and opportunity work together. It is my goal to empower children. I take that responsibility seriously. Every day I see children who are not living up to their potential. I see it on the streets. I see it in the schools. I see it at the grocery store. I call you to action! My friend often reminds me to seize the day, and I ask you to do the same. Seize this day and make a commitment...a commitment to children...a commitment to success.

You have read the book. You have felt the emotion that empowered you to finish it. Now find a child.

Drop to your knees and tell that child how much you love him or her. Look that child in the eyes and let him know that, right now, he is the most important person in the world. Let him know you care. Put this information to work, NOW.

There is an old Chinese proverb which says:

When you hear something, you forget it.
When you see something, you remember it.
But not until you do something will you understand it.

Do you want to empower a child? Then give that child something that can never be taken away. Not a toy or a game, but something he'll have the rest of his life. Teach him or her something—anything. Give him the power to be successful, the power to say yes and the power to say no. Give him the power to learn and the power to forget, the power for compassion, and the power for discipline. Give him or her the power to embrace the needs of others and the power to protect. We all have the ability to empower. Make smart choices. Set high standards, and you, too, can live your dreams. Good luck.

"When I was a boy of fourteen, my father was so ignorant I could hardly stand to have the old man around. But when I got to be twenty-one, I was astonished at how much he has learned in seven years."
—Mark Twain

Afterword

I wrote *The Art of Empowering Children* out of my passion for children and my desire to help others. At times I come across as being black and white concerning my techniques, but I'm always willing to change and to learn more. Different philosophies are everywhere, and I challenge you to create your own.

This is not a parenting book, but a teaching book. I have not covered how to raise children, only how to teach and empower them. I have held nothing back, sharing both my victories and defeats. As always, growth never stops, and over time, wisdom increases. Teaching is just a skill, a skill that must be practiced and refined.

I would be grateful to hear from you. I would like to know what does and doesn't work for you. Although I can't guarantee your success, those who have a desire to be better and to make their students better will succeed. Rise every day and move forward. Picture the perfect life for yourself and your students. A friend of mine always tells me, "No one's perfect." I'm the type of person who responds with, "Why not?" Be that type of teacher—one who asks, "Why not?" and then makes it happen.

Change material possessions into life experiences. Give back more than you take, and never stop teaching.

Bibliography/ Recommended Reading

Armstrong, Thomas, *The Myth of the A.D.D. Child* (Dutton, 1995).

Awaken the Giant Within (Simon and Schuster, 1986).

Bandler, Richard and Grinder, John, *Frogs into Princes* (Real Press, 1989).

Blanchard, Kenneth and Johnson, Spencer, *One Minute Manager* (Fontana, 1983).

Brooks, Michael, *Instant Rapport* (Warner Books, 1989).

Miller, George, The magical number, seven plus or minus two: Some limits on our capacity for processing information. *Psychological Review*, 63, 81-97.

O'Connor, Joseph and Seymour, John, *Training with NLP* (Thorsons, 1994).

Robbins, Anthony, *Unlimited Power* (Simon and Schuster, 1991).

Structure of Magic, Vol 1. and Vol. 2 (Science and Behavior Books, 1975, 76).

Trudeau, Kevin, Kevin Trudeau's *Mega Memory* (America Memory Institute, 1989).

Wood, Andrew, *How to Make it Big in America* (Prima, 1995).

Ziglar, Zig, *The Secrets of Closing the Sale* (Berkley Books, 1984).

About the Author

John C. Graybeal holds a Bachelor of Science degree from Illinois State University in Normal, Illinois. He is a former F-16 pilot who graduated number one in his pilot training class. Currently he flies C-130s for the Peoria Air National Guard. He is a fourth degree Black Belt Master Instructor and a former United States Tae Kwon Do Champion. In 1993 he opened a martial arts school in Bloomington, Illinois and began teaching full time. He enjoys working with children and adults through his unique martial arts programs. He can be seen on his own local martial arts television show, *Martial Arts America*. He is very active in children's issues, organizing and raising money to sponsor children in physically empowering programs.

He is a contributing writer to *Martial Arts Professional* and *Martial Arts Business Information Magazine*. As an amateur magician, Mr. Graybeal has performed in venues nationwide including the Flamingo Hilton in Las Vegas.

In his free time, he enjoys working with his bird dog, Lacey, and putting the finishing touches on his first novel, an adventure/espionage thriller about jet fighter planes and the CIA.

How to Contact the Author

John C. Graybeal provides consulting services for organizations, associations, and people who work with children. Requests for information about these services, as well as inquiries about availability for speeches and seminars, should be directed to the address below. Readers are also encouraged to contact the author with comments and ideas for future editions.

John C. Graybeal
1407 N. Veterans Parkway
Bloomington, IL 61704
(309)663-5425
(888)663-9565
e-mail jcgraybeal@aol.com
www.empwr.com

John C. Graybeal's Project Empower Children's Foundation

John C. Graybeal's *Project Empower* Children's Foundation is a non-profit 501 (C) (3) organization formed to do one thing, fund programs that physically empower children. Programs offer martial arts, dance, gymnastics, educational outlets, and guidance to any and all children in need. Our programs are based on the idea that by physically empowering children, we are able to create successful members of society. All programs are built on the foundation of "children first." If you would like more information about the programs offered or funding for your program, please write to:

John C. Graybeal's
Project Empower Children's Foundation
1407 N. Veterans Parkway
Bloomington, IL 61704

Order Form

If you would like to order additional copies please fill out the form below.

Name: _____

Address: _____

City: _____

State: _____   Zip _____

Phone Number: (   )   _____

                              Total number of Copies

Empowering Children $14.95 each _____

IL Residents Sales Tax $1.05 each _____

Shipping and Handling $3.00 each _____

TOTAL $ _____

VISA/MASTERCARD Number _____

Exp. Date: _____

Name on Card _____

Fax your order to (309)663-9565
Call us at (888)663-9565
Or visit our web site at www.empwr.com